WILD ABUNDANCE

RITUAL, REVELRY & RECIPES OF THE SOUTH'S FINEST HUNTING CLUBS

WILD ABUNDANCE

RITUAL, REVELRY & RECIPES OF THE SOUTH'S FINEST HUNTING CLUBS

EDITED BY SUSAN SCHADT

PHOTOGRAPHY BY LISA BUSER

A COOKBOOK ANTHOLOGY

JOHN BESH	DEREK EMERSON	ALEX GRISANTI
KAREN CARRIER	KELLY ENGLISH	DONALD LINK
JOHN CURRENCE	MARTHA FOOSE	LEE RICHARDSON

PUBLISHED BY ARTSMEMPHIS

ADDITIONAL TEXT BY
JULIA McDONALD AND SUSAN SCHADT

RECIPES EDITED BY MIMSIE CRUMP

Shawee Stelly has been working at the Bayou Club for 17 years. A guide and field hand, he gets hunters to blinds, calls in ducks and "makes
sure people have a good time." Chaoui (Shawee) is a Cajun French name derived from the Choctaw *shaui*, meaning "raccoon."

FOREWORD BY SUSAN SCHADT

Editor | President & CEO, ArtsMemphis

Wild Abundance is a salute to the best of the sporting South and celebrates the unique culture of hunting clubs. Avid outdoorsmen, conservationists and hunters embrace a brand of camaraderie steeped in tradition that inspires intense devotion to the land and wildlife, as well as the desire to share it all with family, friends and future generations. The special spirit of such excursions extends beyond the hunt and into the clubhouses and kitchens where memories are made. Blending photography, stories and recipes, this cookbook celebrates the gift of food, the precious bounty derived from preparing meals with care and the relationships and legacy of our Southern culture.

Through the voices of some of the South's most renowned chefs, *Wild Abundance* captures and pays tribute to the heart and soul of nine clubs – the often-untrained cooks and guides who provide comforting sustenance, create traditions and nurture the vitality of each club. Throughout the decades they have become members of the clubs' extended families, integral to creating a sense of home and belonging.

In spite of their fast-paced schedules, every "celebrity chef" gave their time, energy and heart to see this project through to completion. They embraced the vision instantly; they insisted on paying tribute to the cooks and guides on these pages. One is struck by the passion and enthusiasm in their stories, plainly visible through photographs and so well captured through their compelling text – the spirit of abundance come to life.

Repeatedly similar themes arise – the purity of simple preparations, the respect for nature's bounty, the comfort in an embrace or warm smile and the unmatched joy of camaraderie around the table. So many of the chefs speak of being "brought back home," reminded of the comforts of their grandmothers' houses, uncles, hunting trips of their youth and the warmth of friendships past. And each leaves their club having gained something– a new technique or favored recipe, friendships formed and cherished memories.

Wild Abundance would not have been possible without the club members and owners who were so open to sharing their clubs, stories and hospitality with us. Several had been a part of our 2008 publication, *First Shooting Light*, and knew that we were embarking on a project with the utmost respect for their cooks, their land and their traditions. Others from across the South trusted us; their immediate commitment and generosity to the vision inspired the chefs and us and demonstrated a profound desire to honor those who help make their coveted retreats so special.

Through images and the perspectives of nine chefs, we chronicle and celebrate traditions and stories that are truly special. Since the beginning of time, in all cultures, food has been the centerpiece for family and cultural life – the ritual and revelry that we celebrate in these pages.

INTRODUCTION BY TOMMIE DUNAVANT

Co-Chair, *Conservation through Art* | Chair, *Women in Camo*

The journey that led to the creation of *Wild Abundance* began six years ago when ArtsMemphis and Ducks Unlimited first partnered to plan and present the *Conservation Through Art* (CTA) initiative. What started as a celebration around the Federal Duck Stamp competition's move to Memphis after a 70-year history in Washington, DC, has grown and flourished in ways we could not have imagined in 2005. With unprecedented volunteer leadership, CTA has raised more than $2.5 million for the arts, environmental education and wildlife conservation and has allowed us to present free family events, lectures, art exhibitions and scholarships throughout our region and beyond.

In 2008 ArtsMemphis published *First Shooting Light: A photographic journal reveals the legacy and lure of hunting clubs in the Mississippi Flyway*, which elicited a positive and encouraging reaction from conservationists, photography collectors and readers interested in the unique culture of the Mississippi Flyway. I had always known special bonding takes place in the duck blind when people hunt together, and I loved seeing it documented in the book. This bonding carries inside each club with drinking, eating and laughing. It is around the table, as well as in the blinds, that stories are made.

I am proud to be a part of CTA and am excited about the publication of *Wild Abundance*. For some time we had wanted to find a way to involve individual women in *Conservation Through Art*. Many women I know not only support their husbands in their hunting endeavors, but also hunt themselves. The two ideas came together – *Women in Camo* could be a special group of women interested in art and conservation who make a unique contribution. That dedicated group of 101 women has done a remarkable job of supporting our efforts, and I applaud them for helping to make *Wild Abundance* possible.

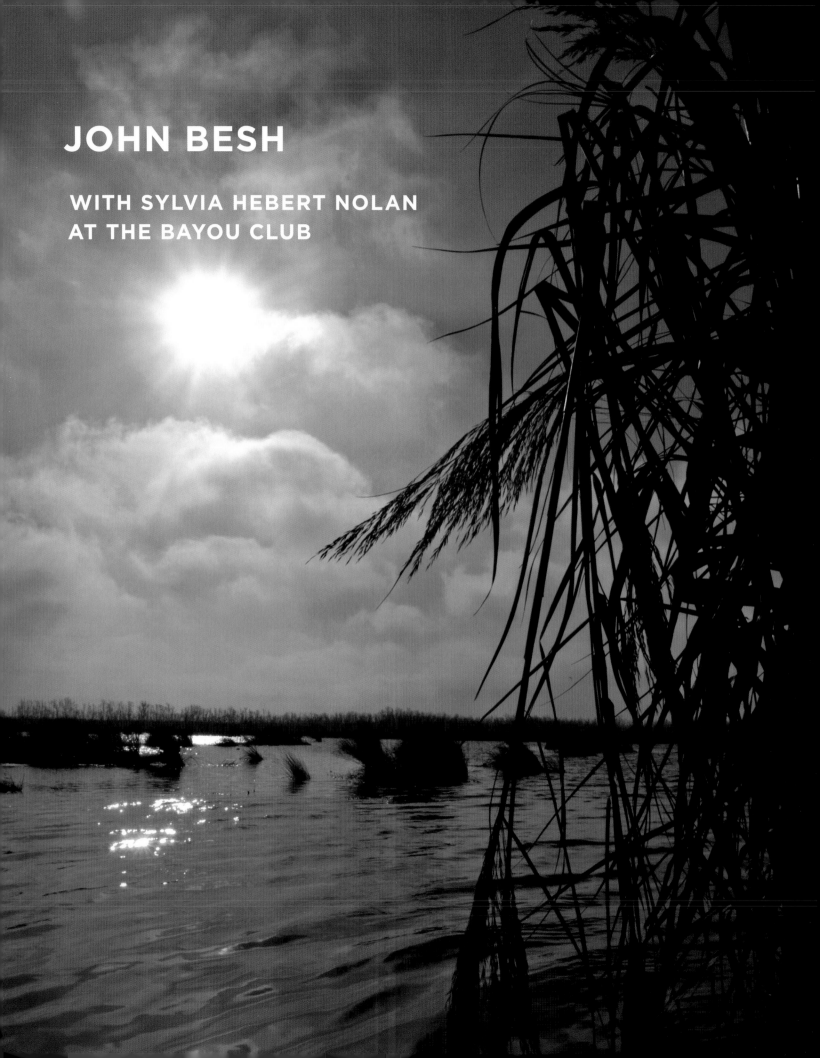

JOHN BESH

WITH SYLVIA HEBERT NOLAN
AT THE BAYOU CLUB

AS LIGHT GENTLY APPEARS OVER THE MARSH, the salty Louisiana sky is barely illuminated and does not yet reveal the teal birds that quickly buzz just yards overhead. Only the high-pitched whoosh of their wings flapping in unison tells us who they are. I sit with the biggest grin on my face. Too early to shoot just yet, I wait in restless anticipation of the first birds to decoy. The dog next to me, quietly moaning, is no more at ease than I for the chance to get after the ducks today.

GUIDES CHAD KOCH AND DARIUS "BIG D"
Girouard ready the duck blind. Earlier in the morning, Mr.
Paul had chatted in French with their confrère Shawee Stelly
("Chaoui," the Native American/Cajun word for "raccoon").
I've been up for hours now. It all started this morning at
about four o'clock, when a porter entered the room and
proclaimed a loud, "Good morning, Mr. Besh. The weather
is partly cloudy with a 60 percent chance of precipitation.
The winds are out of the west northwest and it's presently
40 degrees Fahrenheit," followed by, "breakfast will begin
promptly in 30 minutes, and will you be drinking your coffee
black today?" As on any day of hunting, I quickly jump to
my feet and into my camouflage, which I'd laid out the night
before just after dinner, as if I were a boy all over again.

The funny thing is every time I hear the words "Bayou
Club," I revert back to my early days as a young kid, with
butterflies thinking of what the hunt will hold for me. On
this trip I'm joined by my best friend, brother-in-law and
hunting partner, Patrick Berrigan, who is just as giddy as I
about an opportunity for the hunt of a lifetime and all the
joie de vivre that accompanies such an excursion. Patrick
and I grew up hunting in those lean years of the late 1970s
and early 1980s when we had the point system. Patrick and
I both depended upon shooting a mixed bag, or what we
affectionately call "the white trash grand slam," consisting
of any lower pointed duck that would both fill the bag limit
and bring us a morning of fast action wingshooting. In
general I'm speaking of those species that were frowned
upon by my fancy friends in places like the Mississippi
Delta, who'd never think of shooting grey ducks (gadwalls),
spoonbills, dogris and so forth, but it was what we knew
and what we had plenty of. Our form of duck hunting was
an arduous one that required commitment, paddling a
pirogue for 45 minutes while wearing waders, with a large-
headed, gregarious black lab perched in the front along with
a heavy bag of decoys – so very different from how we'd
hunt on this special trip.

You see, the Bayou Club is much more than just a place to
hunt. It's about ceremony, tradition, camaraderie and, of
course, the best hunting of south Louisiana. The day before,
we started early, loading up the truck with our duffel bags,
shot bags, shotgun cases and bourbon whiskey as a gift
for Mr. Paul McIlhenny, our host and great-grandson of
Edmund McIlhenny, the founder of the Tabasco® brand.

THE BAYOU CLUB

THE BAYOU CLUB, due south of Intracoastal City,
Louisiana, dates back to 1927. Its members, from all over
the country, bring guests to enjoy fantastic duck hunting,
fishing for redfish and shooting skeet on a five-stand clay
target range. The Bayou Club is a marvelous place for its
members to entertain. On this particular trip, "John Besh
was really my guest. The fact that he cooked was a great
lagniappe," said Paul McIlhenny, President & CEO of
McIlhenny Company, the makers of Tabasco® products.

JOHN BESH

EACH OF JOHN BESH'S six acclaimed New Orleans
restaurants – August, Besh Steak, Lüke, La Provence, The
American Sector and Domenica – celebrates the bounty
and traditions of the southern Louisiana region. He is the
host of TLC's *Inedible to Incredible*, and has appeared on
top programs on the Food Network and the Sundance
Channel. His cookbook, *My New Orleans,* was nominated
for a 2010 James Beard Award, and he won the James
Beard Award for Best Chef: Southeast in 2006. *Food &
Wine* named him one of its "Best New Chefs," and his
flagship restaurant, August, was featured on *Gourmet's*
"Guide to America's Best Restaurants," and "America's Top
50 Restaurants."

SYLVIA HEBERT NOLAN

SYLVIA HEBERT NOLAN has been cooking at the Bayou
Club for four seasons, preparing meals for members,
guests and visitors. One of 10 children, she learned to cook
from her mother, aunt and grandmother. Raised in Erath,
Louisiana, Sylvia started her professional cooking career
at age 12, helping her aunt in the kitchen of the town's only
restaurant, Menard's. She went on to cook at fast food
restaurants, nursing homes and a hunting club outside
of Gueydan, Lousiana. Sylvia and her husband live in
Abbeville, Louisiana, and she is the mother of three girls.

Attentive and willing Sylvia Hebert Nolan learns proper trussing technique from the master chef himself.

We met Mr. Paul at Shucks! oyster restaurant in Abbeville, where we consumed with vigor as many oysters as possible. Duck season and oysters are a natural combination; both enjoy the peak of their season together. What better way to kick the trip off than with an oyster feast before heading to the docks of Intracoastal City, where we'd catch the crew boats waiting to shuttle us to Bayou Club, heaven in the marshy estuaries of extreme south Louisiana.

During most duck hunts in south Louisiana, the conversation always comes down to food. This trip is no different. Small talk leads to a serious discussion regarding food and what wines to serve with seemingly predictable foods. I say predictable because our duck season will always pair nicely with gumbo (duck gumbo at that). Since we'd been enjoying oysters all afternoon, we figure why stop there when we can add a few to the duck gumbo for supper. Appetizers should always begin with seafood like beautiful, plump, large white shrimp prepared any number of ways and, of course, boudin, our indigenous pork, green onion and rice sausage, which we consume steamed and fried as well. Crabs are normally in short supply during our colder months, but that doesn't mean we won't pay a little extra for the jumbo lump crab meat that yields a magical salad when tossed with a simple ravigote sauce and served with chicory lettuces and toast points. Paul's only real request/demand is that I debone and stuff whole teal with duck foie gras and roast the birds to a perfect medium rare, which is what I intend to do.

Before we finish the conversation about what's for dinner, the boat slows and takes a hard left into a narrow canal in the marsh that reveals the ancient buildings that comprise the Bayou Club, a club that has stood the test of time, weathering hurricane after hurricane. It's by far not the fanciest group of buildings I've ever seen, but the setting and the romance of hunting at Bayou Club is priceless. As the boat arrives, we are greeted by a team of hunting and service professionals who quickly unload the boat and escort us to the main house, where we're assigned rooms

and made drinks. Just as ducks go with gumbo weather, whiskey (in particular Pappy Van Winkle®) is this trip's drink of choice at the hunt club, served with just an ice cube or two. While enjoying a beverage, we huddle together and discuss the rules of the hunt before I'm off to the kitchen.

I meet up with the beautiful and sweet ladies who I will cook with tonight – in particular Ms. Sylvia, who is quite the chef and leader of this kitchen brigade. Having met Sylvia before, I know she's a pistol and that this is *her* kitchen. Without a doubt, she is able to cook as well, if not better, than most restaurant chefs throughout south Louisiana. As with most folks from Cajun country, she was born not with a silver spoon but one made of wood, perfect for stirring a cast iron pot. Though I had met her before, today will be my first time cooking with her, and boy, am I excited. I come bearing gifts of crabs, oysters, shrimp and wine. That's the way in with a good cook – food and wine! From that point on, we have a ball. We swap stories of gumbo, étouffée, grillades and jambalaya. I pour her a glass of wine and ask her to sit, as I am going to do the work for her tonight. Of course, she won't hear of it. So we get in there and cook, drink and dance. It is on. First things first, I show her how to debone the teal while keeping the skin intact, stuff the birds and prepare them for roasting. While that's taking place, I've also got a sauce made out of quince preserves that will reduce down with onions, cane vinegar and veal stock. I burn the sauce twice, much to the enjoyment of my dear chef Sylvia, who laughs and thinks it humorous that even with a television cooking show, I still burn the sauce. With the stuffed teal in various stages of preparation, the ladies and I work on a few hors d'oeuvres for the hunters to enjoy before the meal. As they wait for dinner to be served, they browse the meticulously kept hunt log, where much speculation is made of where we should hunt and what we might expect to bag.

Shucks! owner David Bertrand (right) welcomes (l to r) Patrick Berrigan, Paul McIlhenny and John Besh.

David Bertrand shows John Besh and Mike Fitzpatrick the storage shed for live, fresh oysters.

Once everyone has had their fill of bam bam shrimp, fried oysters with Louisiana caviar ranch dressing, rabbit boudin balls and various pâtés and terrines of wild game, it is time to enter the dining room, say grace and sit down to our salads of crab ravigote, duck and oyster gumbo, whole roast foie gras stuffed teal with quince, wild mushrooms, spaetzle and the best bread pudding on earth. Conversation at dinner is consumed by talk of the upcoming hunt and, of course, what the breakfast menu might look like. After dinner, it is one last toast and then off to bed, where I spend a sleepless night mentally preparing for the first flight of teal to light into our spread of decoys. What kind of fellow can sleep on a night like this? For fear of oversleeping, I wake every hour, on the hour, check the time and then return to dreams of French ducks and speckled bellies.

Once awake and dressed, we all meet at the living room table and gather around the American flag to consume our "orange sandwich," consisting of a wedge of orange and a shot of 23-year-old Pappy Van Winkle bourbon, followed by singing *God Bless America* with enthusiasm. We enjoy a hearty breakfast of fluffy biscuits, bacon, sausage, creamy grits, eggs and coffee that's as dark and rich as the night's sky. It's off to the gun room to pick up the shotguns and shells that we'll certainly need on this wonderful day. We load our guns as shooting time approaches, and Patrick and I begin our finest day of duck hunting ever on this 30,000-acre parcel of marshland paradise that's home to millions of wintering waterfowl. Moments later it's on, six teal over the decoys and six teal bagged. What a start to such an unforgettable day. Yes, life is good – and even better at the Bayou Club. ❁

"It's by far not the fanciest group of buildings I've ever seen, but the setting and the romance of hunting at Bayou Club is priceless."

A gift of Pappy Van Winkle® calls for a mischievous laugh.

Chief guide Robert Guidry welcomes (l to r) Took Osborn, Patrick Berrigan, John Besh and Mike Fitzpatrick to Bayou Club.

Club manager Bruce Wade (standing) enjoys "tall" table tales. (clockwise from l) Cortney Viglietti, Susan Schadt, Chuck Thomason, Mike Fitzpatrick, Paul McIlhenny, John Robertson, John Besh and Took Osborn

Bayou Club cook, Sylvia Hebert Nolan

The pride of culinary accomplishment: chef, cook and club member savor a job well done.

FOIE GRAS
STUFFED DUCK

JOHN BESH

SERVES 8

What's not to like? Perfectly roasted duck with the bones carefully removed and stuffed with fatted duck liver, better known as foie gras. Creating this dish must be a lot like getting to heaven; it will take commitment, but the result is miraculous.

NOTES:

The wild mushroom stuffing will complement the liver while also helping absorb all of the delicious juices rendered from both the duck and the liver during the roasting process.

The brioche included in the stuffing helps absorb the excess liquid so the stuffing will bind but not become dense.

Trussing allows the stuffing and the bird to stay intact and lets the bird cook in a very uniform manner.

Foie gras is available at specialty food retailers like Hudson Valley Foie Gras.

- 8 WHOLE TEAL DUCKS
- 4 TABLESPOONS BACON GREASE (OR OLIVE OIL IF DESPERATE)
- 1 ONION, CHOPPED
- 4 CLOVES GARLIC, CHOPPED
- 1½ POUNDS WILD MUSHROOMS, SLICED
- 3 CUPS BRIOCHE, CUBED
- SALT & PEPPER TO TASTE
- 1 TABLESPOON THYME, CHOPPED
- 2 TEASPOONS SAGE OR ROSEMARY, CHOPPED
- 1 CONTAINER FOIE GRAS
- NUTMEG, FRESHLY GRATED
- 8 SLICES PROSCIUTTO
- 4-6 TABLESPOONS OF RENDERED DUCK FAT OR OLIVE OIL

DEBONE THE TEAL by removing the backbone and gently cut down both sides to remove the ribcage while keeping the skin attached to the flesh. You should end up with one solid piece of breasted duck with the skin side down.

In a large sauté pan over medium heat, soften onion in bacon fat or oil until golden brown, stirring frequently. Add garlic and mushrooms and cook until liquid is released and mushrooms are softened. Add the brioche and remove from the heat. After a couple of minutes when the mixture has set slightly, season with salt, pepper and herbs.

Slice the foie gras about ¼ inch thick and season each slice with salt, pepper and nutmeg. Place a slice of prosciutto on each duck, then a slice of the foie gras, and top with a heaping tablespoon of the stuffing. Gently roll up the teal and secure it with butcher's twine.

Preheat the oven to 500 degrees. Season the outside of the birds with salt and pepper. Heat the duck fat or oil in a large pan over high heat and sear the ducks until a deep, mahogany brown. Top with additional herbs if desired. Place the ducks in the oven and cook for about 7 to 10 minutes until no more than medium, and allow them to rest several minutes before slicing.

Grilling duck poppers, a favored ritual at Bayou Club: (l to r) Paul McIlhenny, Darius Girouard, Chad Koch, Chuck Thomason and John Besh

BAYOU CLUB
BAM BAM SHRIMP

SERVES 4-6 AS AN APPETIZER

I like to think of these as fried shrimp with the sauce included. Just toss the crispy shrimp in the spicy mayonnaise glaze until each shrimp is lightly coated, and you'll understand just how addictive these can be. It's all about eating what is local. I'm amazed that the same marsh system that gives refuge to millions of wintering waterfowl is also home to our enormous shrimp fishery.

- 1 POUND JUMBO SHRIMP, PEELED & BUTTERFLIED
- 1 CUP CLUB SODA, COLD
- ¼ CUP RICE FLOUR
- ½ CUP ALL-PURPOSE FLOUR
- ½ TEASPOON SALT
- 1 TABLESPOON TABASCO® SWEET & SPICY PEPPER SAUCE
- ¼ CUP GOOD QUALITY MAYONNAISE (I LIKE BLUE PLATE® MAYONNAISE)
- CANOLA OIL TO DEEP FRY

PREHEAT OIL to 350 degrees in a large sauté pan. Mix together club soda, flours and salt. Place shrimp into batter and remove each one, making sure excess batter has dripped free from shrimp before placing shrimp into oil. Once golden brown, remove shrimp from oil and drain on paper towels. In a mixing bowl, combine pepper sauce and mayonnaise. Add fried shrimp to the mixing bowl and toss so that each shrimp is lightly coated with mayonnaise glaze. Serve immediately.

24 THE BAYOU CLUB **WILD ABUNDANCE**

Hunting manager Walter Wainwright, guide Chad Koch and Paul McIlhenny plan
the morning blind assignments with added sustenance from John Besh.

DUCK POPPERS

JOHN BESH

SERVES 4-6 AS AN APPETIZER

These duck poppers inevitably show up in one form or another all around south Louisiana duck camps. Since they're made of ingredients that every camp has, it's no wonder they are so prevalent. At Bayou Club, Darius Girouard usually makes the duck poppers, and we shared recipes and this task. They are easy and delicious, no matter what species of duck you happen to use.

NOTES:

We use this recipe with many meats, such as squab or venison.

Be sure not to cook the duck beyond medium rare; it tends to be dry.

Don't cook the duck skewers in advance; have them ready for the grill, and cook when you're about to serve.

- ¼ CUP SUGARCANE VINEGAR OR BALSAMIC VINEGAR
- 2 TEASPOONS SUGAR
- 2 SHALLOTS, MINCED
- ¾ CUP CANOLA OIL
- 3 TABLESPOONS PECAN OIL
- SALT TO TASTE
- FRESHLY GROUND BLACK PEPPER TO TASTE
- 2 WHOLE BONELESS, SKINLESS MALLARD OR PEKIN DUCK BREASTS, SLICED ACROSS THE BREAST INTO STRIPS ABOUT ½ INCH THICK
- 6-9 STRIPS BENTON'S SMOKED COUNTRY BACON OR OTHER THICK-CUT BACON, CUT IN HALF CROSSWISE
- 4 OUNCES CREAM CHEESE
- 3 PICKLED JALAPEÑOS, THINLY SLICED LENGTHWISE

- 12 6-INCH WOODEN SKEWERS, SOAKED IN WATER FOR 30 MINUTES

WHISK VINEGAR, sugar and shallots together in a large bowl; gradually add oils, whisking constantly. Season marinade with salt and pepper. Add strips of duck to the bowl and let them marinate for 30 minutes.

Lay a piece of bacon out on a clean work surface. Place a strip of duck on top of the bacon. Add aproximately 1 teaspoon of cream cheese on top of each duck strip, then top with a piece of jalapeño. Season with salt and pepper. Wrap bacon around duck and jalapeño and slide a wooden skewer through to secure. Repeat the process with remaining bacon, duck and jalapeños, seasoning each with salt and pepper. Discard the marinade.

Prepare a charcoal or gas grill. Meanwhile, wrap ends of the skewers with aluminum foil to protect them from burning while on the grill. Grill duck skewers until bacon crisps and has rendered its fat and duck is cooked medium, 5 to 7 minutes.

The night before the hunt, Paul McIlhenny demonstrated the sure-shot technique for the next morning, saying each hunter should pick out a single bird, bring the gun firmly to his cheek and swing through. Paul's shooting technique has been perfected, as evidenced the next morning when he shot a "triple" – three shots taken, three teal down.

DUCK GUMBO

SYLVIA HEBERT NOLAN

SERVES 6

I always cook gumbo the same way, but sometimes we might put in other things like andouille and sausage and oysters – it depends on what you have, what you want in it. When I started working at the Bayou Club, Mr. Walter, hunting manager at the camp, came in and helped me figure out exactly how to make it as the club members like. I have to thank him if I'm going to talk about gumbo.

NOTES:

Depending on the size of your pot, you may need to brown ducks in batches.

Chopped smoked sausage, shrimp and oysters all make great additions to this gumbo. Sausage will take 20 minutes to cook in the gumbo, oysters 15 minutes and shrimp 5 minutes.

- VEGETABLE OIL
- 14 WILD DUCK BREASTS
- DASH OF SALT
- DASH OF BLACK PEPPER
- DASH OF CAYENNE PEPPER
- DASH OF GARLIC SALT
- DASH OF TONY CHACHERE'S® ORIGINAL CREOLE SEASONING
- 2½ CUPS MIXED VEGETABLES, CHOPPED (LIKE PARSLEY, GREEN ONION, ONION, BELL PEPPER & CELERY)
- 1½ CUPS FLOUR
- 1 CUP VEGETABLE OIL
- 1 TEASPOON GUMBO FILÉ
- DASH OF TABASCO®
- GREEN ONIONS, CHOPPED (FOR GARNISH)

LIGHTLY COVER the bottom of a big pot with cooking oil over medium high heat. Season duck breasts with salt, black pepper, cayenne pepper, garlic, salt and Creole seasoning. Place duck breasts in the pot, letting them brown well on all sides but remaining slightly pink in the middle (this might take 30 minutes). Remove from pot.

Add mixed vegetables and sauté until softened and lightly browned. Add ducks back to the pot. Add enough water to cover.

In a saucepan, mix flour and oil to make a roux. Cook over medium low heat, stirring constantly, until the color of chocolate. This could take up to an hour. Whisk roux into the pot with ducks. Add gumbo filé and Tabasco®. Let simmer for 2 to 4 hours, adding additional water if needed. Serve over rice.

Sprinkle with chopped green onions for garnish.

As (l to r) Mike Fitzpatrick, Paul McIlhenny, Sylvia Hebert Nolan and Patrick Berrigan get a cooking "class" from John Besh, Robert Guidry watches from a safe distance.

(l to r) John Besh, Celina Vincent and Darius Girouard

Guide Darius Girouard, affectionately known as "Big D," reluctantly accepted a taste of John Besh's fried oyster garnished with what he only knew as duckweed. "Not so bad after all."

POTATO SALAD

SYLVIA HEBERT NOLAN

SERVES 10

I learned to cook potato salad from watching my mama and my aunties cook growing up. I serve potato salad on the side of gumbo, but a lot of people in south Louisiana like to add it to their bowl of gumbo.

- 6 LARGE WHITE POTATOES, PEELED & CUBED
- 3 EGGS, HARD BOILED
- 2-3 TABLESPOONS PICKLE RELISH (SWEET OR DILL)
- 1 TABLESPOON ONION, MINCED
- 1 TABLESPOON BELL PEPPER, MINCED
- 2 TABLESPOONS YELLOW MUSTARD
- MAYONNAISE
- SALT & PEPPER TO TASTE
- PAPRIKA FOR GARNISH

BOIL POTATOES in salted water until tender, approximately 10 minutes. Drain and smash potatoes, leaving some lumps. Chop eggs and add them along with pickle relish, onion and bell pepper. Add mustard and enough mayonnaise to even out the texture of the potato salad. Season with salt and pepper.

Sprinkle a little bit of paprika across the top to add some color.

STRAWBERRY SAUCE

SYLVIA HEBERT NOLAN

YIELDS APPROXIMATELY 1½ CUPS

I started as a housekeeper at the Bayou Club and would watch Roy, the former farmer/cook, in the kitchen. He used to say, "You'd better watch because you might have to do this someday," not knowing it would come true! I picked up some hints and some recipes from him, including this strawberry sauce that I usually serve over pound cake. I'll drape it over the cake and top with whipped cream.

- 1 POUND STRAWBERRIES
- ½ CUP WATER
- ½ CUP POWDERED SUGAR
- 1 TABLESPOON GRANULATED SUGAR

CORE AND SLICE strawberries. Add them to a saucepan with water and both sugars. Cook strawberry mixture over low heat for 30 minutes, or until strawberries are broken down. Cool and serve over cake or ice cream.

As Mike Fitzpatrick, Paul McIlhenny and Took Osborn sit down to dinner,
Tiffney Huntsberry Green and Chad Campbell proudly serve Sylvia's potato salad.

Pre-morning ritual: "God Bless America with gusto!" Paul McIlhenny, Chuck Thomason, John Robertson, Took Osborn (great-grandson of Edmund McIlhenny) and John Besh

(l to r) Patrick Berrigan, John Besh and Paul McIlhenny

As the windy morning hunt progressed, there were many excellent shots taken. Upon the rare occasion of a missed shot, the conversation became quite lively and often humorous. As Chef Besh took aim at a pair of teal ducks and missed his quarry, he declared, "Good thing about that wind is they come in slower; the bad thing is they leave faster."

Instantly the perpetually entertaining Paul McIlhenny regaled the group with the following*:

"A pair of teal over the marsh
Low and slow they flew.
John Besh jumped, shot thricely
And got all but two."

*Paraphrase of a 1921 Bishop Alexander poem presented to then Bayou Club president, Edmund McIlhenny, in the late 1960s by the late Jack Stibbs, Dean of Academic Affairs at Tulane University. Stibbs had seen the poem at John F. Maybank's plantation, Lavington, south of Charleston, South Carolina.

Best friends, brothers-in-law and hunting partners Patrick Berrigan and John Besh

Mike Fitzpatrick and Chuck Thomason share a celebratory fist bump in the blind.

An 1857 Theodore Sydney Moise portrait of family patriarch Edmund McIlhenny

Pepper mash is fermented and aged in old, oak bourbon casks for three years.

Hamilton Pope displays aged pepper mash on Avery Island.

Our trip to the Bayou Club included a tour to the world-famous Avery Island and McIlhenny Company, maker of Tabasco® brand products. McIlhenny Company is still privately owned by the same family that founded the company in 1868. Family patriarch Edmund McIlhenny planted the first red pepper plants on Avery Island, Louisiana, in the 1860s and went on to invent the famous Tabasco® sauce. McIlhenny Company continues to manufacture Tabasco® sauce right where it all began, on Avery Island. Many McIlhenny employees reside on the island and descend from previous generations of company employees. Each workday the Tabasco® factory produces hundreds of thousands of bottles of sauce, which are labeled in 22 languages and dialects and sold in 164 countries and territories around the globe. Little could Edmund McIlhenny have realized over 140 years ago that his homemade condiment called "Tabasco®" would become a pop culture and culinary icon – the most famous, most preferred brand of pepper sauce in the world. As the product's vintage slogan declared, "There is only one TABASCO®!"

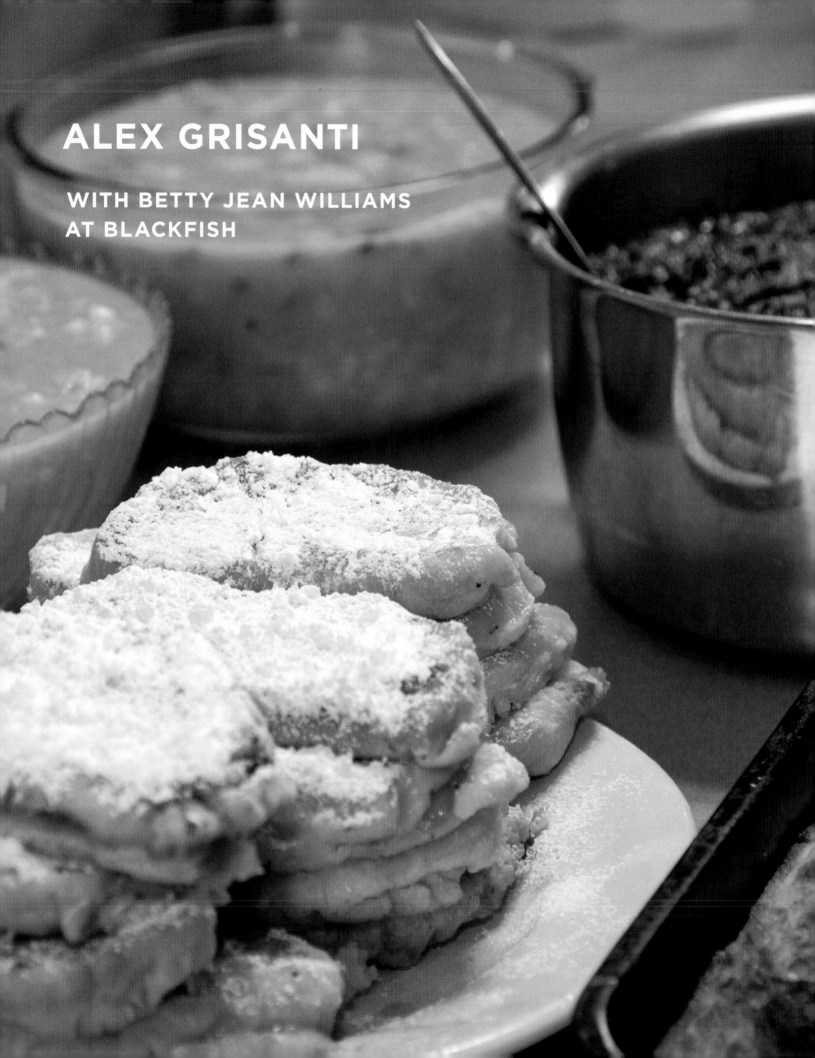

ALEX GRISANTI

WITH BETTY JEAN WILLIAMS
AT BLACKFISH

HUNTING, FISHING & COOKING have been my whole life. If I'm not in my kitchen, I'm crappie fishing or deer hunting with my boys. It's a very vital part of my life, and I enjoy it immensely. Growing up, I'd go hunting with a buddy and his dad. The minute I turned 16 I'd go wherever I could find a spot and just set up camp. I'm showing my age, but we used to go to Sardis Lake in northern Mississippi, and there wouldn't be one duck hunter out there. We'd just go out there, bust a hole in the ice, sit on the side of a tree and shoot ducks. It's just a way of life for me. I love to be out there with my son; we'll spend three or four days in the woods. It's good stress relief – no telephones, no TVs. I love to rough it. I'll get some big trophy buck, and someone will ask where I shot him. I'll say, "I stalked him down in the river for five days." I really love everything about hunting.

LAST MAY my family celebrated 100 years of being in Memphis, and we have always been in the restaurant business. Men like Blackfish members Billy Dunavant and John Stokes have been lifelong customers and friends. Prior to this trip, I had been to Blackfish several times to hunt with those guys, and I already knew what a wonderful person Betty Jean is. She's got a great personality. She speaks out and she loves when the hunters come in and start telling the stories. They don't edit themselves in front of her. Betty Jean has been there for 30 years, and she loves those guys. Blackfish is a phenomenal place. The duck hunting is probably some of the best in the world. When you have the best people helping you cultivate, telling you what to plant and how tall the water is, you've got perfect conditions. That's what Mr. Billy and Mr. Stokes strive for – perfect conditions every day of duck season.

You'd think titans of industries would all have fancy lodges. But Blackfish is very modest when you drive up. The kitchen in the clubhouse is not big at all; you can hardly turn around in there. My granddaddy used to say, "You couldn't cuss a cat in there without getting a mouthful of hair." On this trip I went straight to the kitchen, where Betty Jean already had most of the cooking done. She sits over that food like a mother hen. She and her daughter Valra Selvy stew over that food. They've got to touch it and keep reorganizing it. She'll resort the chicken, move the cornbread around. It's like the more you touch it, the better it's going to taste.

I think a lot of times the perception of the non-hunter is that at duck clubs, people mostly eat game. There may be a game dish cooked every now and then, but usually you come in at night and they have pot roast or steaks or pork chops. The members at Blackfish look forward to Betty Jean's staples – Southern comfort food like fried chicken, turnip greens, chicken and dumplings and peach fried pies. I relate well to people like Betty Jean because cooking for them has been an everyday way of life, a necessity to sustain their families. You get guys like John Stokes or Billy Dunavant, who could eat anywhere in the world, and this is like gourmet food to them. To Betty Jean, it's survival food. It's cheap, comfort

BLACKFISH

BLACKFISH HUNTING CLUB sits on 1,500 acres in Crittenden County, Arkansas. Founded in 1978, it is owned by a group of four Memphis businessmen and one former Memphian in Houston. The three-bedroom clubhouse at Blackfish can sleep eight, though many times members will hunt in the morning and then make the short, 30-minute drive back to Memphis. Because of this, lunch is the primary meal served at Blackfish, and members often leave with a to-go bag of Betty Jean Williams' Southern cooking specialties.

ALEX GRISANTI

ALEX GRISANTI is the chef/owner of Elfo's Restaurant in Germantown, Tennessee. He carries on a century-old tradition of northern Italian cooking by the Grisanti family in Memphis. For years, he worked with his father at Ronnie Grisanti & Sons, consistently named one of the best Italian restaurants in local competitions. Among his honors, Alex was invited to cook at the James Beard House in New York City in 2001. He studied culinary arts in Italy and is a certified American Culinary Federation chef. He holds degrees in nutrition from Johnson & Wales University and in pastry arts from the Culinary Institute of America. An avid outdoorsman, he serves on the board of the Tennessee Wildlife Federation.

BETTY JEAN WILLIAMS

BETTY JEAN WILLIAMS is the manager and cook at Blackfish Hunting Club, where she has been preparing meals for its members for 30 years. She grew up the eldest of 10 children in Stuttgart, Arkansas. A self-taught cook, she always loved food and cooking for her family. Having grown up picking cotton, she worked for three years operating an air hammer on interstate road construction; she has also driven a tractor, planted beans and driven an 18-wheeler. "Hard but honest work" has been the cornerstone of Betty Jean's adult life, which included raising 13 children.

Betty Jean keeps watch over her culinary "charges."
(l to r) Billy Dunavant, John Stokes, Alex Grisanti,
Woodson Dunavant and Andrew Phillips

food that could feed a lot of people and put meat on their ribs. That's what she had to do growing up. She had to feed her husband and 13 kids. She told me that 20 years ago there wasn't a market down the street for her to run to and grab something when everyone was hungry. She used to raise her own chickens, ducks and turkeys for the eggs. She still grows a lot of food in her garden – squash, okra, purple hull peas, tomatoes, peppers and turnip greens. I think it's neat that guys who are so successful gravitate to food like hers for that comfort. It's almost like a mom taking care of a bunch of kids. You get those guys around a table and they're fighting for a peach fried pie. "Don't eat the last one! Split it with me!"

Betty Jean just sits in that kitchen and holds court over her food. As she puts it, "I never cook by a recipe. I cook by my brain. I know just what to put in to make things right." Her fried chicken is awesome. I'm surprised she doesn't soak it. I asked if she did a buttermilk or ice bath, and she said no, she double rolls it in flour. She wouldn't really get to the recipe with me; I kept trying to pull it out of her. I got from her the basic flour, pepper, garlic salt and chicken. She just slow fries it and gets a nice hearty, moist crust on the chicken. She says John Stokes' favorite part of the chicken is "the last part that goes over the fence. He would jump out of an airplane for that tail!" She makes her greens the same way I do. She puts a ham hock in the pot to start making her turnip greens, which she grows herself. When Betty Jean was growing up and teaching herself to cook, they had no elaborate seasonings. They had ham hocks, ham bones, sugar, salt, pepper and onions. They didn't have an array of spices. To do what she's doing in her recipes, I guarantee you she uses no more than four spices for everything. That's her way of cooking and her way of life. Her chicken and dumplings are awesome. Hers are very traditional. She boils her chicken with celery and onions. She pulls it, makes her dough and boils the dough in the stock of the chicken. The trick with the dumpling is you can't leave it in that chicken stock forever, or it will start disintegrating. You have to be really careful. Dumplings are probably one of the trickiest

"Betty Jean just sits in that kitchen and holds court over her food. As she puts it, 'I never cook by a recipe. I cook by my brain. I know just what to put in to make things right.'"

things in the world to make. Not many people home-make them, and they're labor intensive. Betty Jean's fried pies are great. Hers are fluffy and big and have a lot of dough around the edges. Gosh, I could eat some right now! She cooks absolutely everything in that tiny clubhouse kitchen and says "that one small kitchen will cook more than you can bring in here!" She's there at four o'clock in the morning, ready to fix breakfast, and she says the hunters "don't ever have to wait on me to finish cooking."

Mr. Billy asked me to make a D&G Salad – the Dunavant & Grisanti salad. It's chopped iceberg lettuce, black olives, mortadella, prosciutto, bacon, tomatoes and crumbled bleu cheese with a vinaigrette called Miss Mary's dressing. Mr. Billy and my dad came up with that salad together, and it's on the menu at my Italian restaurant, Elfo's. Some of the members asked me to cook and serve one of my lobster pizzas when I was over visiting Blackfish. I also made a white pizza with portobello mushrooms, roasted tomatoes, goat cheese and grilled chicken. For dessert I made cannoli. I wrapped the dough around wooden dowels and threw them in the fryer. After I pulled them out, I let them cool for a minute; the dowels started to shrink down and the dough came off a little bit. I just pulled the dough off and filled them with a sweet mascarpone mixture to make classic cannoli.

Blackfish is really a special place. They have some great mounts decorating the walls and hanging from the ceiling. The members love to tease each other and poke at each other. Henry Morgan doesn't push and prod as much as Mr. Stokes and Mr. Billy do, but he's got a great sense of humor. Mr. Stokes can hold court, he and Mr. Billy both. The more they talk, one gets louder than the other. There's a really convivial spirit at that club, whether the guys are out in the blinds or sitting around the table enjoying one of Betty Jean's meals. The members really love her. They are protective of her and show her genuine affection. Over the years she went from picking ducks to cleaning and cooking to now being the cook and manager of the club. She's proud of her position, and those guys think a lot of her.

Cooking and eating are such an important part of hunting for me. I eat every piece I catch or shoot. I love to cook wild game. We eat all the venison, the ducks, the doves and the crappie. At my hunting club, Caulk Island, a couple of the guys and I cook lunch and dinner every day. It's a lot of fun. Hunting, fishing and cooking – for me it just doesn't get any better. ✿

Alex Grisanti sets to work at the simple but effective Blackfish bar.

The famous Dunavant & Grisanti salad

DUCK BOLOGNESE

ALEX GRISANTI

SERVES 4-6

This dish always reminds me of our Italian hometown, Lucca. It is a traditional live-off-the-land dish. You can put almost any game meat or vegetable in this dish. You can always continue to add ingredients to this pot for several days. Eating this duck Bolognese is so comforting, it feels like your mother just gave you a hug.

- ½ CUP LARD OR OLIVE OIL
- ½ POUND MILD ITALIAN SAUSAGE
- 1 POUND DUCK BREAST, SLICED
- ½ YELLOW ONION, DICED
- 2 CARROTS, DICED
- 2 CELERY RIBS, DICED
- 1 CUP WHITE MUSHROOMS, SLICED
- 2 CUPS CANNED WHOLE TOMATOES
- 1 CUP WHITE WINE
- 4 CUPS CHICKEN STOCK
- ½ CUP TOMATO PASTE
- 1½ CUPS MILK
- 1 TABLESPOON FRESH SAGE
- ⅓ CUP PARMESAN CHEESE
- SALT & PEPPER TO TASTE

HEAT LARD or oil in a large pot over medium high heat. Brown sausage and duck breast in lard or oil, breaking up sausage with a wooden spoon as it cooks. Remove meat and set aside. Add vegetables (onion through tomatoes) to the pot and cook until softened, approximately 5 minutes. Add white wine and put meat back into pot. Add chicken stock, tomato paste, milk, sage and Parmesan cheese. Bring to a boil, then reduce heat to simmer for several hours. Season with salt and pepper to taste.

Serve over your favorite pasta.

SLOW COOKED RUTABAGA

ALEX GRISANTI

SERVES 4

Rutabagas are a nice alternative to turnips. This recipe goes well with all varieties of wild game. Vernon Butler, the real cook at my deer camp, showed me this recipe. It is a favorite comfort food of mine, and we always cook it on deer hunting trips because our wives can't stand the smell at home.

- 1 LARGE RUTABAGA, PEELED & DICED
- ½ YELLOW ONION, DICED
- ½ CUP LARD OR VEGETABLE OIL
- ⅓ CUP SUGAR
- SALT & PEPPER TO TASTE

PUT ALL ingredients in a double boiler or slow cooker on low heat. Slow cook for several hours until very tender.

SPINACH UOVA

ALEX GRISANTI

SERVES 6

- ¾ CUP OLIVE OIL
- 2 POUNDS FROZEN SPINACH, THAWED, WELL DRAINED & CHOPPED
- 1½ TABLESPOONS GARLIC, MINCED
- 7 EGGS, LIGHTLY BEATEN
- SALT & PEPPER TO TASTE
- 1 PINCH NUTMEG
- ½ CUP PECORINO CHEESE, GRATED

HEAT OLIVE OIL over medium high heat in a large sauté pan and add spinach. Add garlic and cook until softened. Add eggs, salt, pepper and nutmeg and stir constantly until eggs are barely set. Fold in pecorino cheese and serve immediately.

WHITE BEAN STEW

BETTY JEAN WILLIAMS

SERVES 6-8

Betty Jean's white bean stew includes a surprising ingredient, sugar. She says her secret is to add sugar to everything she cooks. In this recipe, sugar smooths out the flavors, or "takes the whang out of it," as Betty Jean says.

- 1 HAM HOCK, BONE-IN
- 1 POUND DRIED WHITE BEANS
- 3 CLOVES GARLIC, CHOPPED
- 1 YELLOW ONION, CHOPPED
- 1 GREEN BELL PEPPER, CHOPPED
- SALT & PEPPER TO TASTE
- 1 10-OUNCE CAN RO*TEL®
- 1 TABLESPOON SUGAR

PUT HAM HOCK and beans in a large pot and add enough water to cover by 2 inches. Boil ham hock and beans until the beans turn slightly pink, approximately 30 minutes. Add garlic, onion, bell pepper, salt, pepper and RO*TEL®. Simmer until they are softened, approximately 30 minutes. Add the sugar and cook for 10 more minutes. Thin with water, if needed.

PEACH FRIED PIES

BETTY JEAN WILLIAMS

MAKES 4 PIES

FILLING:

- BOILING WATER FOR RECONSTITUTING
- 16-OUNCE PACKAGE DRIED PEACHES
- ½ CUP SUGAR
- ½ CUP PLUS 2 TABLESPOONS WATER, DIVIDED
- 2 TABLESPOONS CORN STARCH
- ⅛ TEASPOON NUTMEG

POUR ENOUGH BOILING WATER over peaches to cover them and let sit for approximately 15 minutes. Drain peaches and place into a saucepan with sugar and ½ cup water. Cook over medium heat until peaches are tender and liquid is almost completely reduced, approximately 10 minutes. Whisk together cornstarch and 2 tablespoons water in a small bowl. Add cornstarch mixture to peaches and stir vigorously with a wooden spoon. Sprinkle nutmeg into peaches and stir, mashing peaches with the wooden spoon as you stir. Set peaches aside to cool slightly.

PASTRY:

- 1½ CUPS SELF-RISING FLOUR, PLUS EXTRA FOR ROLLING
- ⅓ CUP BUTTERMILK
- ⅓ CUP VEGETABLE OIL

- VEGETABLE OIL FOR FRYING
- POWDERED SUGAR TO DUST PIES

SIFT FLOUR into a medium mixing bowl and push it to one side of the bowl. Into the other side of the bowl, pour buttermilk and vegetable oil. Gradually stir the mixture together until it is combined. Knead the dough with your hands until smooth.

Roll dough out onto a liberally floured surface to approximately ⅛ inch thick. Using a sharp knife or a pizza cutter, cut the dough into four squares. Place two tablespoons of peach filling on one side of each dough square. Fold dough over to cover peaches and press around the filling to release any air pockets. Press edges of the dough firmly with the tines of a fork to seal. Refrigerate pies for 20 minutes.

Heat two inches of vegetable oil in a heavy skillet (such as cast iron) and cook pies for 1 to 1½ minutes on each side, until golden brown. Place cooked pies on a rack to drain and cool. Sprinkle liberally with powdered sugar while still warm.

"The members really love her. They are protective of her and show her genuine affection...She's proud of her position, and those guys think a lot of her."

TURNIP GREENS

BETTY JEAN WILLIAMS

SERVES 6

Betty Jean's instructions start out, "While you're picking your own greens, turn the heat on under your meat…" She has been cooking greens since she was 12 years old and invented this recipe, which the hunters at Blackfish swear are the best turnip greens around. Betty Jean says that smaller is better when it comes to turnip greens; a smaller bunch is tender and has "more good taste."

- 1 HAM HOCK, BONE-IN
- 6-8 BUNCHES OR 3 POUNDS TURNIP GREENS
- VEGETABLE OIL
- SALT & PEPPER TO TASTE
- 2 TEASPOONS SUGAR

NOTES:

To strip the leaves off the turnip green stems, hold the leaf at the top and gently pull straight down the leaf on each side of the stem.

COVER HAM HOCK in 8 cups of water in a large pot. Simmer for 30 minutes until tender. Meanwhile, wash turnip greens thoroughly to remove all sand and grit. Strip the leaves from the stems; discard stems. When ham hock is tender, add turnip greens to the pot. Pour ½ inch of vegetable oil over the greens and add salt and pepper to taste and the sugar "straight down the middle of the pot." Boil for 40 to 45 minutes, until desired tenderness.

CORNBREAD

BETTY JEAN WILLIAMS

SERVES 6

- ½ CUP VEGETABLE OIL
- 1½ CUPS SELF-RISING WHITE CORNMEAL
- ½ CUP FLOUR
- 2 EGGS, LIGHTLY BEATEN
- 1 TABLESPOON SUGAR
- 1 CUP BUTTERMILK
- 1 CUP WATER

PREHEAT OVEN to 350 degrees. Add vegetable oil to an 8x8 baking dish and heat the dish in the hot oven. Meanwhile, mix together cornmeal, flour, eggs, sugar, buttermilk and water. Pour cornmeal mixture into the middle of the hot dish. The oil should seep up at the sides. Spread the hot oil over the top of the cornmeal mixture and allow it to soak in (you shouldn't see the oil any longer). Bake at 350 degrees for 35 to 40 minutes. Move the cornbread under the broiler to brown the top, approximately 2 minutes.

Billy Dunavant and John Stokes, the convivial cut-ups of Blackfish

Daughter Valra Selvy with Betty Jean Williams

Blackfish member Buck Neely sports his trophy duck bands.

"Betty Jean just slow fries it and gets a nice hearty, moist crust on the chicken. She says John Stokes' favorite part of the chicken is 'the last part that goes over the fence.'"

Club member Henry Morgan, back for seconds

Alex Grisanti with Andrew Phillips, nephew of Blackfish member Harry Phillips and grandson of Harry J. Phillips, in whose memory the *Conservation Through Art* celebration dinner was founded

Betty Jean Williams

The Blackfish duck log with the 2010 season tally reflecting that winter's unprecedented freeze

LEE RICHARDSON

WITH KEVIN SHOCKENCY
AT CIRCLE T

Lee Richardson enjoys the solitude and frozen serenity of Circle T.

THERE IS NOTHING ORDINARY about a duck hunt in Jefferson County, Arkansas. And for those fortunate enough to be a guest of Susan and Chuck Smith, a meal at Circle T, right outside Stuttgart, is just as magical as the flyway. ¶ I spent my youth and, to some degree, found my professional calling at a deer hunting camp in Adams County, Mississippi. This place is a long way from the nearest paved road, remote and home to relatively undisturbed herds of deer and wood ducks and the occasional mallard. We had a pretty nice house with running water, some ranges lifted from a hotel in Natchez and plenty of heat. I had always thought of it as a well-outfitted camp. When it came to meals, it was a community affair with a loosely recognized instigator. We were just a bunch of rednecks cooking for ourselves. A visit to Circle T put me in touch with relativity.

ONE IS WELCOMED to Circle T by a lake full of gadwall, three stately lodges and a nicely kept road of oyster shells, and then by Kevin Shockency, a renowned wild game cook and executive chef of the Memphis Hunt and Polo Club. In spite of its beautiful design and thoughtful finishings, Circle T (like Chef Kevin without the overstated white coat and toque) immediately works to instill a casual sense of needlessness. It achieves the sublime effect on mood that might be expected from settling into a '64 Mustang on a Sunday drive down Route 66.

For me, the arrival to camp has always been filled with childlike anticipation: "Who will be here, who won't, who will be new to camp, what has changed, who has bagged what and where should I hunt in the morning?" This moment has always been preceded by an almost year-long, hope-filled ritual of combing outdoor magazines for the best new gear, choosing a breeder, training retrievers and carefully outfitting and packing our bags to protect ourselves from weather's whimsy and the unforeseen. Be prepared! It may also involve choosing the right cigar or remembering to grab the poker chips. It is a process of hedging success in the field and choosing what to share around the table, setting the stage for the year's most longed for R and R.

This particular weekend in mid-January, the weather brought an Arctic front that produced snow at Disney World and iced over most of Arkansas' prime waterfowl ponds, cutting short the season for most hunters by two weeks and certainly dashing our much anticipated hunt in the morning. But, as I said before, the anticipation is childlike; I still packed my shotgun and more than one box of shells!

That inkling of hope that something would turn in the weather delivered all of us, if not just me, to the back door of the main house at Circle T. As guests began to arrive, many entering through the kitchen, I witnessed the same sense of reunion and celebration of times past that I have returning to Mississippi every fall. Some guests had met before, some had not; it was impossible to decipher whether Chef Kevin had been hired or invited. There was something

CIRCLE T

THIRTEEN MILES outside Stuttgart, Arkansas, Circle T is owned by Chuck Smith of Memphis and comprises a compound of buildings and a 75-acre lake, all set on nearly 700 acres. Purchased in 1991, Circle T has become a cherished place for Chuck and his wife, Susan, to entertain. Circle T's large, industrial kitchen comes in handy when preparing meals in a clubhouse that can sleep 22. On special occasions, the Smiths enlist the aid of Kevin Shockency, executive chef of the Memphis Hunt and Polo Club, to create unforgettable meals for their family and friends. When he's in charge of the menu, Shockency creates a theme around each dinner. His thoughtful meal preparation and the Smiths' warm hospitality have made for many a memorable celebration and quite a few rollicking New Year's Eves at Circle T.

LEE RICHARDSON

THE NEW ORLEANS restaurant scene provided Lee Richardson with opportunities to work with and learn from top-notch chefs, including Kevin Graham, Emeril Lagasse and John Besh. Rising to the rank of chef de cuisine at Besh's celebrated Restaurant August, Richardson was led, in the aftermath of Hurricane Katrina, to Little Rock and the Capital Hotel, where he is executive chef. He leads an ambitious culinary tour de force focused on defining Arkansas' place in Southern food through interacting with its seasonal bounty in a style he calls New Americana Cuisine. He has been a three-time semifinalist nominee for the James Beard Best Chef: South and has been featured in several national magazines, including *Food Arts, Garden & Gun, Bon Appétit* and *Gourmet.*

KEVIN SHOCKENCY

KEVIN SHOCKENCY has been executive chef of the Memphis Hunt and Polo Club since 1998. Kevin grew up in Marion County, Kentucky, in a family that fished, hunted, raised cattle, grew their own vegetables and made their own butter. That dependence on locally raised, fresh food has influenced his cooking style ever since. A graduate of the Culinary Institute of America, Kevin has been a chef at several private clubs, including Eagles Landing Country Club in Stockbridge, Georgia; Jennings Mill Country Club in Athens, Georgia; and Jackson Country Club in Jackson, Tennessee.

Partners at the pan: Lee Richardson and Kevin Shockency

(bottom row, l to r) George Dunklin, Jr., Ronnie Owen, Ed Bleazer, Steve Reynolds: (top row, l to r) Chuck Schadt, Lee Richardson, Chuck Smith, Fraser Humphreys, Bryan Jordan and Kevin Shockency

gratifying about such an experience of privilege so devoid of airs. On the "guest list" for years, Kevin, settled into the commercially-outfitted though residential-feeling kitchen as though it were his own, was able to shake hands and offer beer while effortlessly working up the evening's meal and inviting the interested to see and taste the luring preparations.

As our chef, Kevin was more a host and partner, both entertaining guests who wandered into the kitchen and unfolding a meal at the table one surprise at a time. A meal at Circle T is no more ordinary than its surroundings, and it entertains as importantly as it satiates. As good as he may be with coaxing wild critters and beasts from pan to plate, there is nothing rustic about one of Kevin's meals at Circle T. He responded to the ubiquitous cream cheese and duck breast jalapeño popper with a delicate chicken tart, bound with a touch of cream cheese and gentle heat of jalapeño. The lean, strong-tasting wild bird was replaced with a rich terrine and carefully rendered breast of Long Island Pekin. We were tempted with Gulf Coast treasures of big shrimp simmered in a spicy cream and perfectly fried oysters, crispy and soft on a tangy and moistening remoulade; the only reminder of our dreamlike state: the mixture of breading is a Memphis Hunt and Polo Club secret he would not divulge. Even my attention was stripped from this puzzle as Kevin announced the theme of our menu: *Artkansas*!

We became oblivious to the low-teen temperatures. Without notice, attention to time was released as we drifted into a surreal midwinter night's dream. A grand dinner transitioned into the kind of experience that after-dinner drinks were made for. We forgot about the hunt but we still donned some of our gear as we moved outside to the bonfire –hosts, guests, service staff and all. The evening lingered and our morning pushed back. We awakened the next day to enjoy Kevin Shockency's brunch of fried quail, sautéed apples, smothered pork chops and skillet potatoes. This place that sets the backdrop for the magical experience of hunting became an enchanting experience on its own. While Chuck Smith and Circle T couldn't provide the hunt,

they gave instead invaluable time to enjoy the rarity of the surroundings in which we found ourselves. No one missed a thing. We all gained a few of life's most pleasurable hours. What a gift!

As we gathered our things and prepared to return to the real world, packages of ducks, the last to be taken before the season's untimely close, were distributed to each of the guests as gifts in parting. Even without making a hunt, a hunter never leaves Circle T with an empty bag. ✾

"Without notice, attention to time was released as we drifted into a surreal midwinter night's dream. A grand dinner transitioned into the kind of experience that after-dinner drinks were made for."

Chef Kevin "unfolding a meal…one surprise at a time."
In the kitchen: (l to r) Debbie Smith, Cortney Viglietti and Kevin

GOAT CHEESE STUFFED PORTOBELLOS WITH MIXED GREENS

KEVIN SHOCKENCY

SERVES 6

Using local products and seasonal ingredients is the best way to appreciate the full flavors of freshness. Adding different elements to your dishes, like chargrilling the portobellos, then adding the goat cheese and breadcrumbs, then roasting in the oven – all those steps add a little different flavor profile. Everyone can get the same ingredients. It's what you do with them afterwards that will set them apart when you are planning your next dinner menu.

- 6 SMALL PORTOBELLO MUSHROOMS
- SALT & PEPPER TO TASTE
- 2 TABLESPOONS OLIVE OIL
- 1 POUND GOAT CHEESE
- 2 TABLESPOONS FRESH CHOPPED HERBS (SUGGESTED: THYME, BASIL, CHIVES, SCALLIONS OR PARSLEY)
- 1 CUP BREAD CRUMBS
- 1 PACKAGE BABY MIXED GREENS
- VINAIGRETTE

PREHEAT OVEN to 300 degrees. Remove stems from portobello mushrooms. Season with a little salt and cracked black pepper. Drizzle with 1 tablespoon olive oil. Heat a grill or grill pan over high heat. Grill mushrooms on each side for about 4 minutes. Remove and let cool. After mushrooms have cooled, crumble goat cheese on top. Sprinkle with fresh herbs and bread crumbs and drizzle with remaining olive oil. Place on a baking pan. Bake for 20 minutes or until golden brown. Remove from oven and place on a bed of baby mixed greens. Drizzle with your favorite vinaigrette.

Hostess Susan Smith

CHICKEN TARTS WITH JALAPEÑOS

KEVIN SHOCKENCY

MAKES 36 HORS D'OEUVRES

Using simple ingredients, you can create, experiment and try different flavor combinations. I basically created this dish by using simple ingredients we had on hand in the kitchen. The rule of thumb is…there isn't one! Just try the things you like. Don't be afraid to experiment, and enjoy!

- 2 CUPS SMOKED OR COOKED CHICKEN, DICED
- 1 CUP PEPPER JACK CHEESE, GRATED
- 3 TABLESPOON JARRED, DICED PIMIENTOS
- 2 TABLESPOONS JALAPEÑO PEPPERS, DICED
- ½ CUP CANNED CORN KERNELS
- 3 TABLESPOONS GREEN ONIONS, CHOPPED
- 1 CUP CREAM OF CHICKEN SOUP
- 36 SMALL PHYLLO OR TART SHELLS

PREHEAT OVEN to 325 degrees. Mix all ingredients through cream of chicken soup in a bowl until well incorporated. Spoon chicken mixture into tart shells evenly. Bake for 15 minutes. Serve immediately.

NOTES:

These tartlets require minimal culinary effort because smoked or rotisserie chicken is widely available. The filling can be prepared a day in advance and chilled overnight, but do not put in tart shells until ready to bake and serve.

STEWED CINNAMON APPLES

KEVIN SHOCKENCY

SERVES 8

I vividly remember waking up on fall mornings during my childhood, looking out my bedroom window and watching my grandmother picking apples. There was a huge apple tree between my grandparents' house and ours. She would pick all the ones that had fallen to the ground, followed by our daily ritual of peeling and cooking apples. She cooked them every way imaginable, and this was one of my favorites. Thanks, Grandmamma Smith.

- 1½ POUNDS GRANNY SMITH APPLES, PEELED, CORED & DICED
- ½ CUP BROWN SUGAR
- ¼ CUP GRANULATED SUGAR
- 3 TABLESPOONS BUTTER
- 1 TEASPOON CINNAMON
- ½ TEASPOON NUTMEG
- 2 TEASPOONS PURE VANILLA EXTRACT
- ¼ CUP WATER

ADD ALL INGREDIENTS to a stockpot. Bring to a boil and reduce heat to a simmer. Cook for 45 to 50 minutes or until apples are tender. Stir occasionally.

NOTES:

These apples make a perfect topping for the buckwheat pancakes on page 92.

PINEAPPLE CHEESECAKE TART

KEVIN SHOCKENCY

SERVES 8

Everyone enjoys a good dessert. After a great meal, create something that is simple, elegant, light and uncomplicated. Prepare what you can ahead of time – what chefs call mise en place – so all you have to do is assemble the final dish. Practice makes perfect, so keep on cooking!

TOPPING:

- 1 POUND FRESH PINEAPPLE, DICED
- 3 TABLESPOONS HONEY
- 6 TABLESPOONS SUGAR
- JUICE OF 1 LEMON
- 2 TEASPOONS PURE VANILLA EXTRACT
- 2 TABLESPOONS BUTTER

PLACE ALL INGREDIENTS in a medium saucepan. Bring to a boil. Reduce heat to simmer until liquid reduces to a syrup. Remove from heat and chill.

CRUST:

- 4 TABLESPOONS SALTED BUTTER, SOFTENED
- ⅓ CUP LIGHT BROWN SUGAR
- 1 CUP GRAHAM CRACKERS, CRUSHED
- ⅓ CUP OATMEAL, REGULAR OR QUICK-COOKING
- ⅓ CUP ALMONDS, CHOPPED
- ½ CUP FLOUR

PREHEAT OVEN to 350 degrees. Cream together butter and brown sugar. Stir in remaining ingredients and press into a 9 or 10 inch tart pan. Bake for 5 minutes. Remove from oven and let cool.

CHEESECAKE:

- 1½ POUNDS CREAM CHEESE, SOFTENED
- ¾ CUP GRANULATED SUGAR
- ZEST OF 1 LEMON
- 2 TABLESPOONS PURE VANILLA EXTRACT
- 2 EGG YOLKS
- PINCH OF SALT
- 1 TABLESPOON FLOUR
- SWEETENED WHIPPED CREAM OR VANILLA ICE CREAM FOR TOPPING

WHIP CREAM CHEESE and sugar until light and well blended. Add lemon zest, vanilla, egg yolks, salt and flour. Blend until incorporated, scraping down the sides. Pour cream cheese mixture into the pie crust. Bake at 350 degrees for 20 minutes. Remove from the oven and top with cooked pineapple. Return mixture to oven and bake for an additional 25 to 30 minutes. Remove from oven and cool on a rack. Serve with whipped cream or ice cream.

The tart's oatmeal crust, ready for filling

Lee Richardson

Kim Jordan and Chuck Smith sort out which end is up, while Ed Eleazer dons his cap to confront the cold outside.

After-dinner drinks at the fire pit: (seated, l to r) Lilly Humphreys, Ann Reynolds, Susan Smith, Chuck Smith, George Dunklin, Jr., Livia Dunklin, Kim Jordan; (standing, l to r) Ed Eleazer, Steve Reynolds, Fraser Humphreys, Lee Richardson, Kevin Shockency and Bryan Jordan

Chuck Smith shares a story with Ann Reynolds.

Ronnie Owen proudly mans his special domain.

The recipe for Kevin Shockency's fried oysters is a closely guarded secret, one he will not even reveal to Lee Richardson.

CHARGRILLED OYSTERS

LEE RICHARDSON

Kevin Shockency's fried oysters are some of the best I've ever had; the crispy dredge of a great fried oyster is unbelievably elusive. For many people, fried is the most approachable form an oyster can take. The following recipe for doing oysters on the grill is, without a doubt, the single most popular thing I have ever prepared. The rustic simplicity of this divine treat puts years of training in classic cuisine and refined technique to shame.

NOTES:

Gulf oysters should be big and meaty if you can get them. Otherwise, I look for cold water oysters from the East Coast because they are more conducive to shipping by air.

I could probably go into more detail on precise amounts of Parmesan to put on each oyster, or the best ratio of lemon juice to Worcestershire, but that would threaten to disturb the balance of art and science that makes cooking a personal act, a celebration and a sense of hospitality that defines the place in which it comes to life. Call me if you have questions, or better yet, visit me in my kitchen for some personal guidance.

- 1 CUP UNSALTED BUTTER, SOFTENED
- 8 GARLIC CLOVES, MINCED OR GRATED
- 2 DOZEN FRESH OYSTERS
- 4-6 LEMONS, CUT IN HALF
- WORCESTERSHIRE SAUCE
- ¼ CUP GOOD PARMESAN CHEESE, GRATED
- 2 TABLESPOONS PARSLEY, CHOPPED
- 1 BOX KOSHER SALT

PREHEAT THE GRILL and mix together the butter and garlic. Carefully open the oysters without spilling their liquor or damaging the tender flesh with your knife. Discard the top shell and run your knife under the oyster to loosen it from the bottom shell and set aside. Repeat this step until you run out of oysters; you won't have enough!

Place the oysters on the grill and top each with a marble-sized dollop of garlic butter, a dash of Worcestershire sauce, a squeeze of lemon and a pinch of grated Parmesan. Allow the oysters to cook until butter melts and liquid begins to boil in the shell. The key is that the buttery juice will drip into the fire, causing flames to leap up, sort of kissing the oysters and leaving behind a charred flavor that will win over all but the most stubborn of those who think they don't like oysters. I like to finish them with a little chopped parsley and place them on a platter covered with wet kosher salt to keep them from rocking and spilling their precious juice.

DRY CURED DUCK BREAST

LEE RICHARDSON

SERVES APPROXIMATELY 8

I've always had a passion for cured and smoked meats. Fortunately, I've long outgrown Slim Jims and other gas station snacks, but I'll probably never know beef jerky again like it was made when I was a kid in a New Orleans barbecue joint on Magazine Street called Kershenstein's. I will spend the next couple of decades trying to reproduce it. Please, call me if you know these folks. Beef jerky is the gateway to charcuterie, pork its foundation and duck a particular fascination of mine. Like pork and the squeal, you can use just about everything on a duck but the quack. I've even worked on the modified design of a computer controlled "environmental chamber" for my kitchen for curing and aging meats that we affectionately call "the duck box."

Prosciutto is a dry, cured ham of a special pig fed a special diet, raised and processed in and around Parma, Italy, is technically not reproducible. Theoretically, I could import a fresh ham from one of those Italian hogs, put it in my duck box and replicate the weather patterns and ambient conditions of Parma, Italy, in my kitchen in Little Rock for a year and a half to come up with a pretty good approximation, if not a good story. Elusive as prosciutto is, the easiest entry to charcuterie, reproducible to anyone, would be a dry cured duck breast – in layman's terms, duck prosciutto.

- 2 CUPS KOSHER SALT
- ½ CUP BROWN SUGAR
- 1 TABLESPOON COARSELY GROUND JUNIPER BERRIES
- 1 TABLESPOON COARSELY GROUND BLACK PEPPER
- 1 CRUSHED BAY LEAF

- 4 DOMESTIC PEKIN DUCK BREASTS (THOUGH WILD MALLARD BREASTS WOULD BE WORTH A TRY)

MIX ALL ingredients together for the cure. Generously coat duck breasts with the cure and place them in a container just large enough to contain them and the cure without allowing them to touch each other. Cover and refrigerate overnight. Rinse duck breasts to ensure removal of all surface salt (some spices stuck to the meat and skin are okay). Pat dry with paper towels, and wrap duck breasts in two layers of cheesecloth, tying the ends with string. Hang wrapped duck breasts in the refrigerator between shelves in such a way that they are not touching anything else or each other. Leave for 7 days. The duck breasts should feel dense from end to end. If they feel a little squishy in the middle, allow them to hang for another day or two. They will be fine hanging for up to a month. The breasts may then be unwrapped and sliced very thinly. Once cut, they should be consumed within a week.

Lee Richardson's state-of-the-art kitchen
at the Capital Hotel in Little Rock

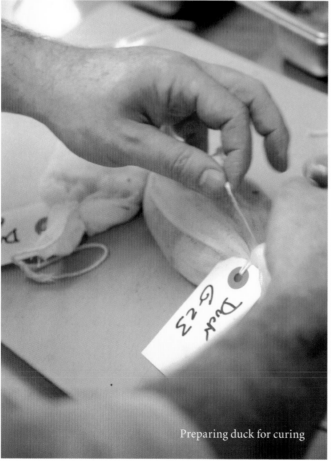

Preparing duck for curing

"Like pork and the squeal, you can use just about everything on a duck but the quack. I've even worked on the modified design of a computer controlled 'environmental chamber' for my kitchen for curing and aging meats that we affectionately call 'the duck box.'"

BUCKWHEAT PANCAKES

LEE RICHARDSON

SERVES 4-6

An old musician friend of the family in New Orleans, John Parker, sings a Cow Cow Davenport song about the allure of buckwheat cakes that seems to have gotten into my head in such a way that I've never forgotten it. I think I've come to learn why. My first experiences in Arkansas involved an introduction to freshly stone ground buckwheat flour from War Eagle Mill and caviar from the paddlefish, harvested a stone's throw from Circle T on the White River. This is a two-tiered recipe, allowing the ambitious to begin by creating a sourdough starter, and the not-so-adventurous to go directly to a traditional batter. Once there, it makes a fine breakfast alongside Chef Kevin Shockency's stewed apples, or a great place to drop a dollop of fine Arkansas caviar with a bit of sour cream. The dish then becomes art mimicking life, as rustic and refined as hunting finds the comfort and companionship of Circle T.

NOTES:

This recipe actually relies on a combination of three factors that contribute to rise and fluffiness in a pancake:

• The yeast fermentation
• An interaction between buttermilk and baking soda
• The beaten eggs

Variations:
For an even fluffier pancake, separate the eggs and whip the whites separately to soft peaks and set them aside while you make the batter. Once the batter is mixed (including the yolks), fold the egg whites into the batter one third at a time.

I like to substitute sorghum for the sugar in the batter recipe to add a little more sophisticated flavor. Cane syrup, maple syrup or molasses would also be good substitutions in the batter.

STARTER:

- ½ PACKAGE YEAST (APPROXIMATELY 1 TEASPOON)
- ½ TEASPOON SUGAR
- ½ CUP WARM WATER (APPROXIMATELY 80 DEGREES)
- 2 CUPS ROOM TEMPERATURE WATER
- 2¼ CUPS BUCKWHEAT FLOUR
- ¼ CUP ALL-PURPOSE FLOUR

COMBINE YEAST, sugar and warm water and allow to stand 10 minutes until yeast are activated. Add an additional 2 cups of water and whisk in the flours until well combined. Leave mixture overnight at room temperature covered with a loosely fitting lid or damp cloth. Feed the starter daily for three days. This means: discard half of the starter and add an additional ½ cup flour and ½ cup water and incorporate. Choosing which flour or combination of flours to feed with is a personal preference. An all-buckwheat flour starter will be very earthy and rustic. After three days the starter should be bubbly and have a pleasant sour smell. The starter may then be used in the pancake batter recipe on the next page, and then refrigerated and maintained indefinitely. To maintain (feed) the starter, take 1 cup out for use or discard and simply add about ½ cup flour and ½ cup water to achieve a wet batter. The starter can be frozen and/or brought back to life after long periods without being fed, but it is good to feed it once a week or so. Over time a liquid will accumulate on the surface that smells a bit like beer. This is called hooch and is perfectly fine. Stir it back in or pour it off depending on the wet/dry consistency of the starter and personal preference of taste. The sourdough technique offers two significant elements to a batter: it lends the distinctive sour flavor that results from the accumulated fermentation as well as the leavening that results from the carbon dioxide produced by the fermentation.

PANCAKE BATTER:

- 2½ CUPS BUTTERMILK
- 2 EGGS
- ½ TEASPOON VANILLA EXTRACT
- ¼ CUP BUTTER, MELTED
- 1 CUP ALL-PURPOSE FLOUR
- 1 CUP BUCKWHEAT FLOUR
- 1½ TEASPOONS SUGAR
- 1 TEASPOON SALT
- ¾ TEASPOON BAKING SODA
- 1 TEASPOON BAKING POWDER
- 1 CUP STARTER (OPTIONAL)

IN A MEDIUM SIZED BOWL, whisk together the buttermilk, eggs, vanilla, melted butter and starter (if using). In another bowl, mix together the flours, sugar, salt, baking soda and baking powder. Stir the dry mixture into the wet mixture until just incorporated. Some lumps are fine.

The batter can be used immediately. However, best results will occur if the batter is allowed to rest 20 or 30 minutes. This allows the yeast to act upon the newly added flour before cooking.

Heat a griddle or large skillet over medium low heat. Add about 1 teaspoon of butter to the pan and, once melted, drop in batter by heaping tablespoons. Cook until lightly browned on the bottom and bubbling around the edges, approximately 3 to 5 minutes. Gently turn and cook until browned on the other side.

Serve immediately or keep warm in a 200 degree oven by placing single file on a towel lined baking sheet.

Kevin Shockency puts the finishing
touches on his Artkansas breakfast.

A comfortable finale: Kevin Shockency
relaxes with Circle T manager Michael Sanders.

DEREK EMERSON

WITH ROSIE MAE BROWN & ANNIE B. HOGAN AT FIGHTING BAYOU

The Lost 40: site of the nightly Benediction

I HAD NEVER BEEN TO FIGHTING BAYOU before, but I certainly had heard of it. A lot of the people from the club have been great customers of ours, and I was excited to visit this place that obviously means so much to them. I don't hunt. I was born and raised in California, where there is not a lot of hunting going on. I've gotten a little bit of an education in hunting and cooking wild game since I've been in the South.

ON THE EVENING OF MY VISIT, I got to Fighting Bayou before Rosie, Annie B. and their helper Bernice. I was shown to my room, and then headed out with the members for their sunset ritual, the Benediction. They call it "paying homage to the ducks." As the sun sinks, the members go to three different spots to watch thousands of ducks gather and settle in for the night. When I returned, the ladies had arrived and were in full swing with the fryers going, the grill going, the ovens on full-tilt. They were working, and I just jumped in and said, "What can I do to help?"

I could tell in the very beginning that Rosie and Annie B. were a little shy. But as we got going, they warmed up to me a lot; they really loosened up. Once they knew I was there to help and I was a part of the group, they let me in. I got them some food and talked to them about cooking. It was like they were thinking, "Maybe you do know what you're doing. Maybe we can learn a little something from you." I don't cook a lot of wild duck, so it was neat to see them soaking it in the milk, pouring the blood out. It was so interesting to see their take on it and what they would do in comparison to what we do in the restaurant. Our game comes in packaged and ready to go. I've done a lot of private dinners for people who will rent the restaurant out and bring their kill – ducks, pheasant, quail. It's fun. We'll do a special menu just for those guys, and it gives me something different to do. Cooking the wild stuff is a lot different, and I love the challenge, learning what works well with the meat.

At Fighting Bayou, Rosie and Annie B. pulled out the duck and the quail, getting ready to fry. For a fried duck appetizer, they cut duck breasts into strips and soaked them in buttermilk. After making a traditional seasoned flour with salt and pepper, they rolled the birds in the flour and fried them in a skillet using peanut oil. I ate a piece of fried quail right out of the fryer ; it was so hot but so good, so crispy. They also prepared a grilled duck appetizer, in which they wrapped applewood smoked bacon around Hoover Sauce-marinated duck breasts. Hoover Sauce comes from a store in Louise, Mississippi, and is the marinade of choice at Fighting Bayou. To me, it tastes like a cross between Worcestershire and barbeque sauce. The Hoover Sauce was perfect, offsetting the gaminess of the duck.

FIGHTING BAYOU

THE FIGHTING BAYOU HUNTING CLUB, which sits on more than 3,000 acres near the Leflore-Sunflower county line in the Mississippi Delta, is the preserve of nine, mostly Mississippi members. The club, which can accommodate 40 guests in its 18 bedrooms, is used not only for some fine duck hunting, but also for engagement parties, family reunions and vacation weekends.

DEREK EMERSON

DEREK EMERSON, executive chef and owner of Walker's Drive-In and Local 463 Urban Kitchen, has elevated the restaurant scene in Jackson, Mississippi. He has won numerous local awards and accolades from such prestigious magazines as *Southern Living*, *Mississippi Magazine* and *Continental Magazine*. Derek was selected as a semifinalist for Best Chef: South in the 2008, 2009 and 2010 James Beard Foundation Awards.

ROSIE MAE BROWN

ROSIE MAE BROWN of Doddsville, Mississippi, has been cooking at Fighting Bayou since 1989. She grew up on a plantation outside Doddsville, where she picked cotton, worked at the grain bin and cooked. A self-taught cook, Rosie's abilities in the kitchen served her in good stead when raising her five children; she now has 13 grandchildren. Hired to cook breakfast for the former owner of the lodge, she has been working at Fighting Bayou since the day its current owners bought the property.

ANNIE B. HOGAN

ANNIE B. HOGAN has also been cooking at Fighting Bayou since 1989. Raised with four brothers in Doddsville, she learned to cook from her mother, a housemaid and cook. Now a resident of Blaine, Mississippi, Annie B. has spent her life and career working on and around farms. While she spends hunting season cooking at Fighting Bayou, she can usually be found working in the fields, driving a tractor. Annie B. has one daughter, who has followed her mother into food service, cooking in a hospital kitchen.

Derek Emerson

Rosie Brown and Annie B. Hogan

Paying homage to the ducks at the Lost 40 – a family affair: (l to r) Hank Burdine, club member Charles Laney, Susan Laney, Karen Bush, Amanda Bush Puckett, member George Lotterhos and Derek Emerson

Charles Bush's grandson, Peyton Puckett

I told Rosie and Annie B. I brought a couple things for them to check out. I tried to bring recipes to Fighting Bayou that they might cook again. They did fried quail, and I made grilled quail with corn salsa as an appetizer. Larry Stephenson, the club caretaker, and I manned the huge grill, cooking the duck to a medium rare and finishing my quail, brushing it with the glaze. A friend of the club had the enormous grill made out of an old, huge propane tank. Larry started cooking on it 10 years ago, and he's become an expert.

Back inside, I made the shrimp toast with aioli, Parmesan cheese, chives and shrimp baked on little baguette slices. Rosie was making green beans and carrots almondine. The kitchen at Fighting Bayou is amazing. They have restaurant-style refrigerators and a stove with six burners and a flattop. It was really fun to cook with Rosie and Annie B. because their personalities are so great. No formal training, but they prepare old recipes that they've been doing for years. Classically trained or not, working with somebody else is always fun. You can always pick something up. You see different tricks. I try to always learn something every day, and it was great to see them doing these traditional favorites, the recipes that the members love so much. The fried quail is a specialty they'll make about once a week. Sometimes they'll grill duck breasts, ribeyes or pork tenderloin, or make fried catfish with turnip greens. Club quartermaster George Lotterhos told me that at one point the club tried to get a little healthier, using more fish and lower-fat foods. Before the end of a week, everyone was pounding their forks and knives on the table, chanting, "We want steak!"

George has been the Fighting Bayou quartermaster from day one, ordering the food and planning menus. Originally, Rosie and Annie B. would only cook breakfast at the club, and the members would go out for dinner or cook meals prepared by George and fellow member Skipper Jernigan. When they built a new, larger clubhouse in 1998, Rosie B. and Annie started coming at night to cook dinner.

The members trained Rosie and Annie B. to make fried quail and some other dishes they really like. In 1999, when the club expanded from 10 to 18 bedrooms, Bernice Davis started coming to help, too – the job just got so big. Sometimes there will be 30 or 40 people there, and someone is hunting five days a week during the season. The ladies are always on hand to make dinner the night before a hunt, and then a huge breakfast in the morning. I could tell how much Rosie, Annie B. and Larry are loved, it didn't feel like they worked there; it was like they were part of the family. They have been there a long time. They know all the kids; they interact with everybody.

The members and guests were having cocktails while I was cooking with the ladies in the kitchen. The food was starting to make its way to the table. They had a buffet set up on a pool table covered with a cloth. Rosie and Annie B. laid out everything, the duck and quail we'd cooked along with vegetables, cheesy grits casserole, salad, garlic bread and rolls. Their clubhouse is huge. You walk into a 50' by 100' room with a pool table, TV and poker table. The kitchen is open to the main room, and hallways come off the main room with several bedrooms. They have a separate house they call the Old Folks' Wing. The original members sleep there, giving up their old rooms to their kids and grandkids. There are bedrooms and bunk rooms, and each family has their name on the door. It's a great thing, so family-oriented. Grandchildren are out running around, it's a heart warming family atmosphere, something I missed growing up in California. You really don't get stuff like that, especially in Southern California or Los Angeles. You just hang out at the beach. It's not quite the same. My family is six people; theirs is 18 rooms full!

Everyone gathered into a circle before dinner was served to say the blessing. George read the menu and introduced me to the group. It was like one big family hanging out. I've seen some of the members and their families since then back in

Jackson – people I'd seen before but didn't really know. Now I feel like I'm part of the family.

George, Skipper, Bubba Tollison and Billy VanDevender all played football with Archie Manning at Ole Miss. Peyton and Eli used to throw footballs out in the driveway at Fighting Bayou when they were young, and they've been hunting there ever since. Eli Manning's football season was over, so he decided to come hunting for the weekend, which I think he does pretty regularly during duck season. I could tell Fighting Bayou is like home to Eli. No one hassles him; no one bothers him. He's just part of the family. It's somewhere he can come, actually relax and have a good time.

The club members have special rituals. I could tell how much they love the tradition and sharing these customs with each other and their families. The similarities to my restaurants routines are apparent, going over the specials with the cooks, discussing the line-up with the waiters, then completing service. The parallels are unexpected and fun. All these things mean so much to them – the Benediction, the pre-dinner blessing and discussion of the menu. After dessert, everyone always goes outside to what is affectionately called the Liar's Pit, where they build a big fire and tell stories. You can tell they've done it for years. Bubba is the real storyteller of the group. If there's a story to be told, Bubba's telling it. He's hilarious. We all just sat around that fire, telling stories and drinking wine. It's obvious why they love being out there so much.

The next morning, I got up early to help Rosie and Annie B. with breakfast while the guys went duck hunting. The hunters went out around six o'clock, and it was absolutely pouring down rain. I stayed in and hung out with the ladies in the kitchen, frying up bacon. When the guys came back, they were just drenched. It did not make me sad that I'm not a hunter. They were gone right at an hour. Three boats full of people came back with everyone having shot their limit. They said shooting started a little late because of the rain. I was standing there cooking, heard "bam, bam, bam," and all of a sudden they were back. They were tearing it up out there.

Rosie and Annie B. laid out a breakfast buffet. Breakfast at Fighting Bayou includes tons of applewood smoked bacon, sausage, turkey sausage, fresh cathead biscuits, green onion gravy, country ham and cheese grits. After eating that awesome breakfast, some members went to nap, some had to head home. Skipper, an attorney, had a deposition that day, so he drove into town, got his work done, came back that night and did it all over again. That's the thing about Fighting Bayou – you just want to keep coming back. The ladies in the kitchen with that great food, the rituals and the way they make you feel at home – it really was a privilege to experience. ✦

Rosie Brown and Derek Emerson talk technique.

The heat is on! Annie B. Hogan laughs as Derek Emerson can't wait to bite into crispy but very hot fried quail.

Skipper Jernigan and Charles Bush, longtime president of Fighting Bayou

Hoover Sauce is a popular condiment at Fighting Bayou. It is sold in just one place – the Lee Hong Co. General Store in Louise, Mississippi. Hoover Lee moved as an infant with his family from China to Louise in 1933, returning to the store his father had established there in 1917. He has been selling his special sauce since the early 1980s. A mix of Deep South and Asian flavors, Hoover Sauce is a spicy but sweet addition to beef, pork, chicken and duck. The recipe is a closely guarded secret, but some say you can approximate the flavor with hoisin sauce, onion powder, minced fresh garlic and chopped fresh cilantro. Having been featured in magazines like *Southern Living* and *Bon Appétit*, Hoover Sauce is available in the quart or gallon by phone order.

Hoover Sauce-marinated grilled duck

QUAIL GLAZE FOR GRILLING

DEREK EMERSON

YIELDS 1 CUP

I learned this recipe from a chef in Atlanta 15 years ago. I took his base recipe and changed it a little bit to make it my own. I tell people at work, "If you're going to steal one recipe, steal this one. It goes with everything." I use it on sturdier fish (tuna, swordfish or salmon), quail, pork chops and pork tenderloin, farm-raised duck and game. It is really a versatile sauce that you should brush gently onto your meat towards the end of your grilling time. You can also reserve some for dipping.

- 1 CUP HONEY
- ½ CUP RICE WINE VINEGAR
- 4 TABLESPOONS SOY SAUCE
- ¼ CUP KETCHUP
- 1 LIME, JUICED
- 1 CINNAMON STICK
- 1 PIECE STAR ANISE
- 2 TEASPOONS GARLIC CHILI PASTE
- ½ TEASPOON GROUND CARDAMOM
- 2 TEASPOONS CORIANDER
- 1 TABLESPOON CRACKED BLACK PEPPER
- 1 TABLESPOON FRESH GINGER, PEELED & CHOPPED
- 4 PIECES CLOVE
- ¼ CUP CILANTRO, CHOPPED
- 1 CHIPOTLE PEPPER IN ADOBO SAUCE, CHOPPED

COMBINE ALL INGREDIENTS in a medium saucepan and bring mixture to a boil. Reduce to simmer and continue to simmer until mixture is reduced by half.

NOTES:

This glaze can be made and held in the refrigerator for weeks.

CORN SALSA

DEREK EMERSON

YIELDS 6 CUPS

This corn salsa started off as a pico de gallo to which I added some roasted corn. It's a little bit lighter, flavor-wise, with lime juice and the vinegar. This is something you can definitely make ahead of time, and it's good on quail or on fish. You can also add black beans and turn it into a dip.

- 3 CUPS FRESH OR FROZEN CORN, THAWED
- 1 YELLOW PEPPER, DICED
- 1 RED PEPPER, DICED
- 1 LARGE JALAPEÑO, MINCED
- 1 SMALL RED ONION, DICED
- 1 CUP CILANTRO, CHOPPED
- 1 LIME, JUICED
- ¼ CUP RED WINE VINEGAR
- 1½ TEASPOONS CUMIN
- 1½ TEASPOONS CORIANDER
- ½ CUP EXTRA VIRGIN OLIVE OIL
- SALT & PEPPER TO TASTE

MIX TOGETHER CORN, all peppers, red onion and cilantro in a bowl. In another small bowl whisk together lime juice, vinegar, cumin and coriander, then whisk in oil. Season dressing with salt and pepper and pour over corn mixture.

Larry Stephenson (l) shares his technique with Derek Emerson. Larry, grill master, has been with the club since 1984. He cooks all meat and game and spends the year readying the property for hunting season.

The blessing: (l to r) Bubba Bounds, Bernice Davis, Annie B. Hogan, Derek Emerson, Rosie Brown and Larry Stephenson

AIOLI & SHRIMP TOAST

DEREK EMERSON

MAKES 36 HORS D'OEUVRES

The topping for this shrimp toast actually started as the crust for an artichoke-and-crab crusted flounder I make at Walker's Drive-In. I needed something for a cocktail party one night, and my wife suggested something on a cracker that could be easily passed around. I'm not a real canapé kind of guy, making a bunch of little tiny stuff. I started out with white bread, spread this cheese and aioli mixture on it and baked it. She said, "It's the best thing I've ever had." It makes a great cheesy, gooey crust. I've probably served it at 100 cocktail parties, and I always get asked for the recipe. You can make it the really easy way – with mayonnaise and cheese – or you can make it the restaurant way with the aioli. It's an easy dish that people love.

NOTES:

The shrimp mixture can be made a day in advance and chilled. Assemble before a party and pop them in the oven a few minutes before service.

AIOLI

- 2 GARLIC CLOVES
- 1 EGG
- ½ LEMON, JUICED
- SALT & PEPPER TO TASTE
- 1½ CUPS OLIVE OIL

COMBINE GARLIC, egg, lemon juice, salt and pepper in a blender and pulse until smooth. Slowly add olive oil in a stream through the opening of the lid of the blender until the mixture thickens and is smooth. Check for seasoning and add more salt and pepper if needed.

SHRIMP TOAST

- 1½ CUPS SMALL SHRIMP (90/110 COUNT), PEELED
- 1½ CUPS AIOLI (OR YOUR FAVORITE MAYONNAISE)
- ¼ CUP CHOPPED CHIVES OR SCALLIONS
- 1½ CUPS PARMESAN CHEESE, GRATED
- A BAGUETTE CUT INTO ¼ OR ½ INCH ROUNDS

BRING A LARGE POT of lightly salted water to a boil. Add shrimp and poach them until they just turn pink. Remove immediately and chill in the refrigerator until ready to use.

Mix aioli or mayonnaise together with chives and Parmesan in a bowl. Gently fold in the shrimp.

Preheat oven to 375 degrees. Spread shrimp mixture on baguette slices and bake until golden brown, approximately 10 to 15 minutes. Serve immediately.

The pool table pulls double duty.

Skipper Jernigan gets a whiff of the powerful hot pepper sauce.

Hank Burdine makes his Rule family recipe for hot pepper sauce, which goes on greens, black-eyed peas or, according to Hank, "If you're like William Faulkner at his deer camp eating his favorite meal, collards and coon." Hank's instructions are as follows:

"Get the biggest, most expensive jug of whiskey you can find.

"Drink all the whiskey except ½ cup.

"Take all the peppers you yourself have grown, including jalapeños, seeded and deveined habañeros, whole Tabasco® peppers, Thai peppers and chiltepíns (if you have them) and put them in the jug. Wear latex gloves or wash your hands 100 times after handling the peppers, 'cause you'll hurt yourself.

"To add color, you can also add red and yellow bell peppers, sliced longways.

"Fill the jug with white wine vinegar. Let it sit for about a month, shaking it every once in a while."

Rosie Mae Brown

FRIED QUAIL

ROSIE MAE BROWN &
ANNIE B. HOGAN

**RECOMMENDED ONE QUAIL PER PERSON FOR
APPETIZER, TWO FOR ENTRÉE PORTION**

Fried quail is a Fighting Bayou specialty that is usually served once a week. The recipe comes from Libba Lotterhos of Jackson, Mississippi, the mother of Fighting Bayou member George Lotterhos. George and his father would hunt quail his mother would then prepare on special occasions. George trained Annie B. and Rosie to prepare some of his favorite dishes, which have become clubhouse favorites.

- 6-8 QUAIL, SPLIT IN HALF
- 2 CUPS BUTTERMILK
- 2 CUPS SELF-RISING FLOUR
- 1 TABLESPOON SALT
- 1 TEASPOON BLACK PEPPER
- PEANUT OR OTHER OIL FOR FRYING

SOAK QUAIL in buttermilk (in the refrigerator) at least one hour and up to 24 hours. Heat oil in a deep fryer or large Dutch oven to approximately 350 degrees. Mix together flour, salt and pepper, and put mixture in the bottom of a large paper sack or zip-top bag. Remove quail from buttermilk, shaking off excess liquid and place in the sack or bag. Gently toss until quail is completely coated. Place coated quail on a wire cooling rack for about 15 minutes before frying to ensure that the crust is set. Fry in batches until quail is golden brown and fully cooked, approximately 4 to 5 minutes.

CHEESY GRITS CASSEROLE

ROSIE MAE BROWN &
ANNIE B. HOGAN

SERVES 8

Every morning at Fighting Bayou features a full breakfast that includes, like any good Southern breakfast, grits. Rosie invented this recipe for cheesy grits casserole to serve as a dinner accompaniment. She makes extra cheese grits in the morning to save in the refrigerator all day. These serve as the foundation for the evening's casserole, often served alongside the fried quail.

- 1½ CUPS GRITS
- ¾ TEASPOON SALT
- 16 OUNCES VELVEETA®, CUBED
- BLACK OR CAYENNE PEPPER TO TASTE
- 3 EGGS, LIGHTLY BEATEN
- BUTTER FOR GREASING THE PAN
- 1¼ CUP CHEDDAR CHEESE, SHREDDED

PREHEAT OVEN to 375 degrees. Cook grits (with the ¾ teaspoon of salt) according to the package directions, and remove from the heat. The grits should be very thick. Stir in Velveeta® and then pepper and eggs. Pour mixture into a lightly greased 9x13 casserole dish and top with shredded cheddar cheese. Cook for 45 to 60 minutes, or until cheese is bubbling and the top is slightly puffed and lightly browned.

The great storyteller Bubba Tollison (in duck shirt) entertains his audience: (l to r) Skipper
Jernigan, Derek Emerson, Peyton Puckett, Charles Laney and Eli Manning.

ROSIE'S BLUEBERRY CRUNCH

ROSIE MAE BROWN

SERVES 8

Years ago Rosie developed this crunch recipe when she worked for a lady who requested a blueberry crisp recipe to serve at parties. When George Lotterhos asked Rosie to prepare a dish that took advantage of bountiful fresh blueberries, she revived the recipe she had created 16 years prior. The two secrets to the crunch's success are to use only fresh blueberries and to keep it in the oven "until it's golden brown, the best in town," as Rosie says.

NOTES:

If blueberries are not available, substitute sliced peaches, plums or nectarines.

- 5-6 CUPS FRESH BLUEBERRIES
- 1 BOX YELLOW CAKE MIX
- ¼ CUP FLOUR
- 1½ CUPS PECANS, CHOPPED
- 1 CUP UNSALTED BUTTER, MELTED
- ADDITIONAL BUTTER FOR GREASING THE PAN

PREHEAT OVEN to 375 degrees. Spread blueberries across the bottom of a greased 9x13 or other large baking dish. Mix together cake mix, flour and butter. Evenly dollop mixture over blueberries. Sprinkle mixture with pecans, making sure to cover the entire dish evenly. Bake for 45 minutes to 1 hour or until the top is deeply browned and bubbling.

Annie B. Hogan

Liar's Pit laughter: Sidney Allen, Bubba Bounds, George Lotterhos (seated), Charles Bush, Eli Manning, Bubba Tollison, Jay Barrett and Derek Emerson

"Fighting Bayou is the best place in the world for unbelievable duck hunting, fabulous Southern cooking and listening to great stories from true characters. I always cherish my time at this special place." – *Eli Manning*

Fighting Bayou has seen its share of notable guests, including the Mannings – Archie, Peyton and Eli. Archie was the teammate of four Fighting Bayou members at Ole Miss, and they have remained lifelong friends. Archie, a native of Drew, Mississippi, has spent many weekends at the club and has been bringing his sons for more than 20 years. Eli joined the hunting on this particular trip.

Contentment all around: Eli Manning and Derek Emerson

Eli Manning, Bubba Bounds, Sidney Allen and Bubba Tollison returning from the hunt, thumbs up

Bubba Tollison, no worse for the weather

Skipper Jernigan and George Lotterhos

Skipper Jernigan and spoonbill

"That's the thing about Fighting Bayou – you just want to keep coming back."

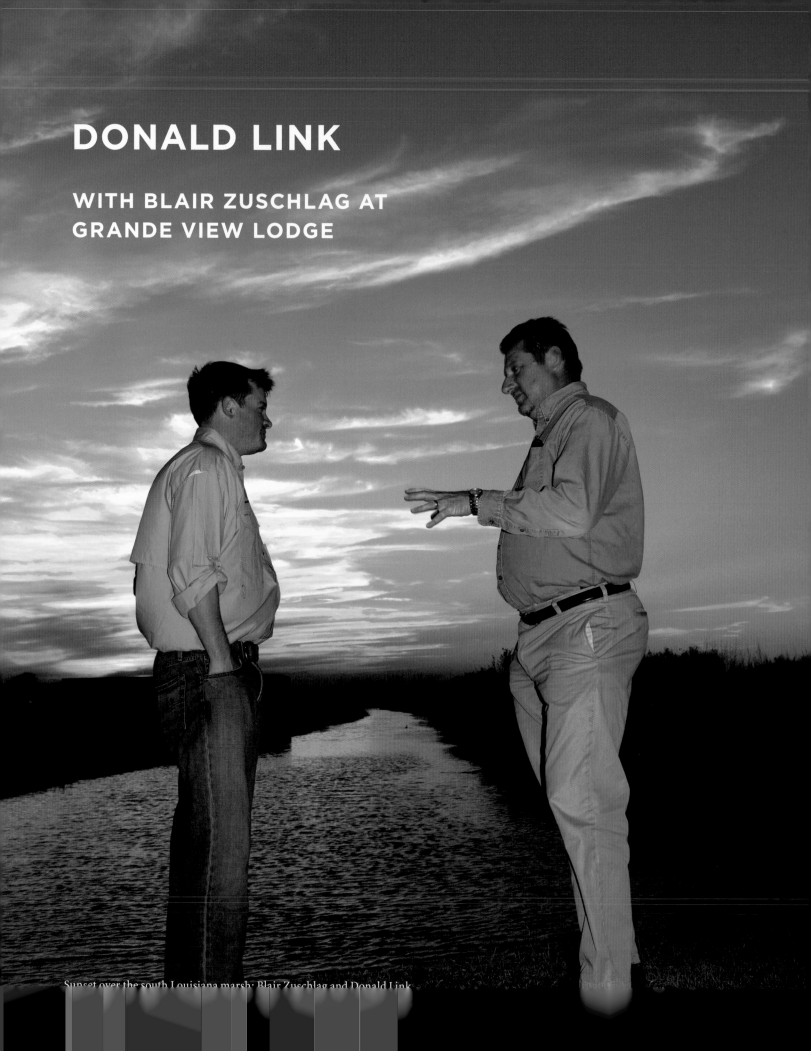

DONALD LINK

WITH BLAIR ZUSCHLAG AT GRANDE VIEW LODGE

Sunset over the south Louisiana marsh; Blair Zuschlag and Donald Link

I'VE GOT TO SAY, I felt very special boarding Richard Zuschlag's private plane to fly to Lake Charles to cook for his hunting guides. That's what Richard does, though – he makes people feel important, from high-powered politicos to chefs to his guides. Richard wanted to pay tribute to these guides, to capture their importance. There are two kinds of guides at Grande View Lodge. The Cajuns, who may be second-, third-, even fourth-generation to farm and raise cattle in that area, know the property the best. That land is in their blood. Other guides are Richard's relatives or Acadian Ambulance medics and paramedics – part-time guides who know the land and love to be out hunting and fishing. The guides are the ones who make the experience happen for Richard's distinguished guests, friends and visitors. Hunting in the marshes can be a daunting experience if you've never done it. I did as a kid, but it has certainly been a long time. Next time I go, I'm going back to Grande View!

BEING JUST SOUTH OF WHERE I GREW UP, I felt right at home in this environment, as if I were in a room of my uncles. The poker, the drinks, the joking around reminded me of my childhood in Lake Charles. This group of guides is so comical and so good to be around. Riding in the boats through the marshes, hearing the familiar sounds of the water splitting and the motor churning was very comforting. To me it feels like a safe place, a place where I belong. These are the places where you can really get to know someone. I can't think of too many situations where I could have had as much of Richard's time as I did on that marsh. We started a conversation that went throughout the day and evening, and now we're good friends in New Orleans. Hunting clubs are about an experience, about bonding – bonding in a way that can't be done over a nice dinner or at a cocktail party. I told Richard and the guides that their relationships with the guests were just as important as the hunting or the meal. You really feel like everyone leaves Grande View as a friend.

We rode through the marshes scouting for ducks. I had heard from others that it was a bad year for Louisiana, but there seemed to be a plentiful supply here. If you have never chased down a flock of ducks in a boat, you should as soon as possible. Their wings skating over the top of the water is a sight indeed. Add in a Louisiana sunset, a cold beer and some good company and you've got a good day on your hands; the kind you wish you had a lot more of.

Coming in from the water, we headed into the lodge to start preparing dinner. Blair Zuschlag and Mac Dupuis set to work cooking ducks. Blair and his cousin Mac enjoy working in the kitchen and wanted to be the ones cooking to show appreciation for all the guides. There is a changing roster of guides who share in the cooking duties. They'll cook anything from ducks to fish to meatball stew. Leighton Guilbeau's dad and uncles taught him to cook seafood gumbo and chicken and sausage gumbo, and he's responsible for cooking at Grande View's annual New Year's Eve Open House for the residents of Creole. Paul Hamilton specializes in preparing baked and fried cheese, special hot appetizers and baked ducks. The industrial kitchen at Grande View is decked out like a restaurant kitchen and gets a lot of use from the guides, guests and big Louisiana

GRANDE VIEW LODGE

SET IN CREOLE, LOUISIANA, Grande View Lodge is the duck hunting lodge of Richard Zuschlag, CEO of Acadian Ambulance. In the heart of Cameron Parish, Grande View serves as a private hunting club and entertaining space as well as a retreat house for Acadian Ambulance management and employees. The lodge, which sleeps 24, is used year-round for duck hunting; offshore fishing for red snapper and redfish; and freshwater fishing for bass, sac-au-lait (crappie) and trout. Renovated in 2007, it includes satellite televisions, Internet connections and a private helipad, making it a hi-tech getaway for personal and company use.

DONALD LINK

DONALD LINK is the executive chef and owner of Herbsaint, Cochon, Cochon Butcher and Calcasieu in New Orleans. His *Real Cajun* was the 2010 James Beard Award winner for best American cookbook. In 2007, he won the James Beard Award for Best Chef: South, and Cochon was nominated as Best New Restaurant. Donald has received numerous accolades from *The New York Times, Travel + Leisure* and *Food & Wine* and was named Best Chef by *New Orleans Magazine*. Herbsaint was featured in *Gourmet*'s "America's Top 50 Restaurants" in 2000 and was inducted into the *Nation's Restaurant News* Hall of Fame in 2009.

BLAIR ZUSCHLAG

BLAIR ZUSCHLAG has taken over increasing kitchen duties at Grande View Lodge over the past three years. He credits his mother and maternal grandfather, both accomplished cooks, with instilling a love of cooking in him and teaching him to do it. A lifelong resident of Lafayette, Louisiana, Blair sells insurance for commercial buildings and operations. However, he is out fishing and hunting "every weekend that I can, as often as I can." An avid outdoorsman, he enjoys cooking game and Louisiana specialties like gumbo for groups of friends and Grande View Lodge guests.

"The kind of day you wish you had a lot more of": Blair Zuschlag and Donald Link

Lodge owner Richard Zuschlag

Cameron Parish resident, part-time guide and always the life of the party, Kim Bourriaque

Donald Link (right) in a room full of "uncles":
(l to r) Leighton Guilbeau, Paul Hamilton, Mac Dupuis
(at stove), Blair Zuschlag and Richard Zuschlag

chefs like John Folse. The dining table just off the kitchen can serve 24, and good meals are a major part of what makes the club special.

As an extra treat for me, it turned out Chef John Folse was there the same night for work on his PBS cooking show, *A Taste of Louisiana*. This was great for me because I have always admired John's cooking and his great love for Louisiana food and culture. Some say that too many cooks spoil the soup, but definitely not in this case. John cooked a smothered duck dish that was truly the best wild duck I had ever eaten. Wild duck can be a tricky dish to cook. It can be dry and gamey if not handled in the right way. These ducks were falling-off-the-bone delicious, covered in an amazing, rich and perfectly seasoned sauce that was the best thing that could have been on top of John's own milled grits. I brought a selection of my cured meats for appetizers, including boudin and some of my favorite smoked duck pastrami, always a crowd pleaser. For a small course I brought a sampling of my slow-cooked pork belly with onion gravy. This was something my Granny used to always make, so I figured it would be great dish to do in Lake Charles. It's not too often that I get to eat so well. I dine all over the world in the best restaurants, but I don't often have those glorious south Louisiana home-cooked meals. I miss them. I miss them more than you can imagine. I can come pretty close to cooking like my grandparents did, but it will never be the same.

I can't say enough about Richard's son Blair and the team of guides. They are fun-loving people who enjoy cooking and hunting and each other's company. After dinner, we piled into boats for late-night frogging, always an adventure. Blair and the guys go out frogging in hardhats mounted with "Cajun-engineered" spotlights to see the frogs. The guides drive the boats in crawfish ponds, which make good habitats for frogs. A lot of people use long stick gigs, but this crew just uses their hands to pull them off trees or out of the water. You've always got to look for the tiny marble white eyes. Don't go after the red eyes – those are alligators! In those ponds it's easy to catch 25 to 100 frogs in one night. Blair likes to cook frog legs or make a shrimp stew, to which he adds a whole frog and lets it cook for a little while.

There were several times in my head on this trip that I was planning on how to leave my "real life" and come back home. This may sound crazy to a lot of people, but there is something extremely peaceful about cruising the waters at night looking for frogs or through the marshes looking for ducks. Just ask Blair, he can tell you. I was so proud to see that group of guides standing in front of the fireplace, so happy that we'd cooked and that Richard had this opportunity to say thanks to them for all their hard work. Those guys are solid citizens who love to take people hunting. If you're ever lucky enough to make it to Grande View, you've got a good time in store hanging out with these guys. Learn to play boo-ray, bring your whiskey and remember there is an ATM on premises if your luck on the table runs out. Richard had one installed when so many of his guests "forgot" their card-playing money and kept asking to borrow his. I only wish I'd been able to stay longer at Grande View – I'm just waiting for my next invitation. ❀

"Being just south of where I grew up, I felt right at home in this environment, as if I were in a room of my uncles."

Wings skating over the Louisiana marsh

The start of a conversation that lasts through the night: (l to r) Guide Kim Bourriaque, Richard Zuschlag and Donald Link

Donald Link, right at home in this environment

SWEET POTATO STUFFED DUCK

BLAIR ZUSCHLAG

SERVES 4

My grandfather, Adley Dupuis, taught me almost everything I know about cooking. We were experimenting one day while cooking ducks, and we happened to have some sweet potatoes. Ready to improvise, I remembered I had heard of someone stuffing a duck with sweet potatoes. I like to brown my ducks as long as possible without burning them. When the ducks are really brown, I'll pour a little bit of water into the pot and let them brown some more. In my opinion, getting them really dark makes the gravy taste better.

- 4 TEAL DUCKS
- CAJUN SEASONING TO TASTE
- GARLIC POWDER TO TASTE
- 2 TEASPOONS YELLOW MUSTARD
- 2 SWEET POTATOES, PEELED & CUT INTO ½ INCH CUBES
- SALT & PEPPER TO TASTE
- 2 TABLESPOONS BUTTER
- 2 ONIONS, CHOPPED
- ½ GREEN BELL PEPPER, CHOPPED
- ½ CAN CAMPBELL'S® GOLDEN MUSHROOM CONDENSED SOUP

SEASON DUCKS WELL inside and out with Cajun seasoning and garlic powder and rub ½ teaspoon of mustard on each duck. Season the sweet potatoes with salt and pepper and stuff into the cavity of each duck. Skewer ducks closed with toothpicks. Chill ducks overnight in the refrigerator, covered.

Heat the butter in a large Dutch oven over medium high heat. Sear ducks on all sides until browned. Remove ducks from the pot. Add onion and bell pepper and cook until softened, approximately 5 minutes. Stir in soup, add ducks back into the pan and add just enough water to cover the birds. Cover, leaving the lid slightly ajar, and cook over low to medium low heat until tender, 1½ to 2 hours. Serve over rice.

"Getting ducks really dark makes the gravy taste better." Blair Zuschlag

The Cajuns know the property best. "That land is in their blood." (l to r) Brett
Baccigalopi, Blair Zuschlag, Donald Link, Richard Zuschlag, Leighton Guilbeau

CHARCUTERIE PLATE: PICKLED ONION AGRODOLCE

DONALD LINK

YIELDS APPROXIMATELY 5 CUPS

For assembling a charcuterie plate, I recommend a varied selection of terrines or head cheese, salamis, sausages and cured meats like mortadella, ham or prosciutto. I suggest including whole grain mustard and pickled cipolinni onions. In general, mustard and almost anything pickled make good accompaniments.

- 3 OUNCES BACON, DICED
- 2 TABLESPOONS OLIVE OIL
- 1 TEASPOON GARLIC, CHOPPED
- ½ CUP SUGAR
- 1 CUP WHITE WINE VINEGAR
- 2 POUNDS CIPOLINNI OR PEARL ONIONS, PEELED

RENDER THE BACON in olive oil over medium heat in a large Dutch oven. Add garlic, sugar and vinegar. Add onions and cook slowly over medium heat until the onions begin to soften slightly, approximately 5 minutes. Serve cold or at room temperature as an accompaniment for charcuterie.

GRITS

DONALD LINK

SERVES 4-6

- 1 CUP STONE GROUND WHITE OR YELLOW GRITS
- 4 CUPS MILK
- SALT & PEPPER TO TASTE
- ½ CUP MASCARPONE CHEESE
- ¼ CUP BUTTER, CUBED

COMBINE GRITS and milk in a medium saucepan and season lightly with salt and pepper. Bring up to a simmer, stirring constantly. Reduce heat to low and cook until milk is fully absorbed, stirring frequently, about 30 to 40 minutes. Adjust thickness with additional milk or water if necessary to reach a nice, creamy consistency. Add mascarpone and butter; stir until fully incorporated. Season with salt and pepper to taste and serve immediately.

SMOTHERED PORK BELLY WITH ONION GRAVY

DONALD LINK

SERVES 6

This recipe was inspired by my Granny's smothered pork. It is also representative of hunter-style dishes my uncles used to make with their kills. The basic principle of the cooking method is to sear the meat, whether it is rabbit, deer, wild hog or duck, then to make a roux and simmer until the meat is tender. Different meats get slightly different treatments. Bacon and mushrooms make great additions to the sauce, as does white wine for lighter-colored meats like rabbit and chicken. For the pork, however, I've always liked the flavor the slow-cooked onions lend to the sauce, especially served over rice or grits.

- 12 PORTIONS PORK BELLY, 2½-3 OUNCES EACH
- SALT
- PEPPER
- THYME
- ½ CUP CLARIFIED BUTTER OR VEGETABLE OIL
- ½ CUP FLOUR
- 2 CUPS ONIONS, THINLY SLICED
- 1 SMALL CARROT, DICED
- 1 TABLESPOON GARLIC, MINCED
- 2 TEASPOONS FRESH THYME, CHOPPED
- 1 TEASPOON CAYENNE PEPPER
- 1 TEASPOON BLACK PEPPER
- 1 TABLESPOON SALT
- 2½ QUARTS CHICKEN STOCK

SEASON PORK BELLY with salt, pepper and thyme. Chill overnight in the refrigerator.

Preheat oven to 325 degrees. Heat butter or oil in a large Dutch oven over medium high heat. Brush the thyme off the pork and sear pork on all sides in the butter or oil in batches; don't crowd the pan. Set pork aside. Add flour to the Dutch oven and stir constantly until you achieve a medium-brown roux, approximately 10 to 15 minutes. Add onions, carrot and garlic, and cook until thoroughly soft. Add thyme, cayenne pepper, black pepper, salt and stock and stir until well combined.

Add pork back to pan, cover and cook at 325 degrees for 3½ to 4 hours.

Serve 2 portions per person over Louisiana rice or grits.

A well deserved pre-dinner tribute to the guides; (standing, front left) Rock Nunez and Kim Bourriaque; (back row, l to r) Manolo Morales, Brett Baccigalopi, Kaleb Trahan, Mitch Baccigalopi, Ricky Canik, Kent Labove, Paul Hamilton and Richard Zuschlag

Blair Zuschlag and Donald Link

Richard Zuschlag played a heroic role in the aftermath of Hurricane Katrina. Responding to the immediate needs of New Orleans hospitals and citizens, he established a first-aid station in the Superdome, created a triage center on the Interstate 10 causeway and dispatched medics who helped evacuate more than 7,000 patients. Acadian Ambulance had the only functioning radio system in the area and had dispatchers, ambulances and helicopters at the ready to aid in rescues. Richard urged state and national politicians to action and coordinated the company's comprehensive support efforts.

Donald Link and Blair Zuschlag

DUCK CONFIT

DONALD LINK

SERVES 4

Duck confit may just be my all time favorite dish, when it's done right. The most exciting element is the crispy duck skin set off by succulent, tender and salty duck meat. Too much salt will ruin it and so will too much cooking. The duck should be cooked long enough so that when you tug on a leg, it gives just a little and feels loose. If you can easily pull it out, it has cooked too long. I test the doneness by gently pressing the middle of a leg where the two bones join. I'm looking to see if it gives just slightly. The beauty of the meat is in its slow cooking. Cooked too fast the meat will get tough and dry. At Herbsaint we leave the duck in its own fat for a couple of days to a week, which gives it time to really sit and develop flavor.

Duck confit is the only remaining entrée from our first menu at Herbsaint, and it will never be removed. The most common duck available in the states is Pekin (not to be confused with Peking Duck). They generally weigh around 4 to 5 pounds. If you are into special ordering, Grimaud Farms and Hudson Valley Foie Gras sell larger legs taken from ducks that are used in foie gras production. These are the ones we use at Herbsaint because of their size and fat content.

NOTES:

There are several different ways to heat this up. Here's my method (the best one): If the duck has been refrigerated, gently melt the fat in a low oven so the legs can be removed. Place them on a glazing rack for about 20 minutes and air dry. This cannot be done with a towel; they must be done this way. Heat a large skillet to medium high heat and add a little duck fat, approximately 1 tablespoon. Gently press the duck leg between your hands so that the skin side forms a flat surface. Carefully place the duck leg, skin down, in the skillet and lower the heat. Put the pan in a 400 degree oven for 7 minutes and do not turn the duck over. This will produce the crispiest duck skin you have ever eaten. It is very important that the meat side of the duck leg never touches any cooking surfaces because it will dry the meat out.

Duck fat can be ordered from online specialty food purveyor D'Artagnan.

- 4 DUCK LEGS (ABOUT 8 OUNCES EACH)
- 2 TEASPOONS GROUND FENNEL
- 1 TEASPOON GROUND ALLSPICE
- 2 TABLESPOONS SALT
- 2 CLOVES GARLIC, SLICED
- 6 SPRIGS FRESH THYME
- 1½ QUARTS DUCK FAT
- OLIVE OIL

DRY DUCK LEGS and season evenly with fennel, allspice and salt. Gently stuff garlic and thyme between the flesh and skin of ducks; cover and chill overnight in the refrigerator.

Preheat oven to 275 degrees. Set legs in a deep roasting pan flat with skin side up. Melt duck fat and pour over duck legs until just covered. Cook covered for about 2½ hours.

Once cooked, use tongs to carefully remove legs to a cooling rack placed over a drip pan. Let cool completely, uncovered. The skin will dry as the legs cool. Preheat oven to 400 degrees. Once legs are dry and cool, use tongs to place them in a hot pan with a little olive oil to crisp up the skin. Sear the skin for about 1 minute over medium high heat and place in the oven for about 4 minutes to warm.

(l to r) Ricky Canik, Mitch Baccigalopi, Rock Nunez and Kent Labove

Richard Zuschlag *is* the king at Grande View Lodge.

Paul Hamilton (left) takes the pot. (l to r) Ricky Canik, Kent Labove, Mac Dupuis, Mitch Baccigalopi and Kim Bourriaque

Bourré – or boo-ray, as it's often known – is a trick-taking gambling card game popular in the Acadiana region of Louisiana. A game for two to eight players, it is closely related to spades and euchre. Like many regional games, the rules of play and betting vary widely. The object is to take a majority of the tricks in each hand and thereby claim the money in the pot. If a player cannot take a majority of tricks, his or her secondary goal is to keep from bourréing, or taking no tricks at all. A bourré comes at a high penalty, usually matching the amount of money in the pot.

CREOLE BRAISED DUCK

JOHN FOLSE

SERVES 4

I first prepared this dish for Bob Kellermann with Lodge Cast Iron at the log cabin at Palo Alto Plantation. It is an old recipe from the Creole kitchens of New Orleans, but when slow braised in a Dutch oven, it takes on new and dynamic flavors.

From *After the Hunt: Louisiana's Authoritative Collection of Wild Game & Game Fish Cookery*, Chef John Folse, Owner & CEO of Chef John Folse & Company, 2517 South Philippe Avenue, Gonzales, Louisiana 70737, www.jfolse.com.

- 6 TEAL OR WOOD DUCKS, DRESSED
- SALT & PEPPER TO TASTE
- GRANULATED GARLIC TO TASTE
- ¼ CUP VEGETABLE OIL
- 1 CUP FLOUR
- 2 CUPS DICED ONIONS
- 1 CUP DICED CELERY
- 1 CUP DICED GREEN BELL PEPPERS
- ¼ CUP MINCED GARLIC
- 1 10-OUNCE CAN DICED TOMATOES, DRAINED
- 1 10-OUNCE CAN RO*TEL®
- 1 10-OUNCE CAN TOMATO PURÉE
- 2 CUPS CHICKEN OR GAME BIRD STOCK
- ½ CUP DRY WHITE WINE
- 1 TEASPOON CHOPPED THYME
- 2 CUPS SLICED MUSHROOMS
- ¼ CUP CHOPPED PARSLEY
- ½ CUP SLICED GREEN ONIONS

PREHEAT OVEN to 350 degrees. Season duck pieces well with salt, pepper and granulated garlic and set aside. In a large Dutch oven, heat vegetable oil over medium high heat. Dust ducks lightly with flour, shaking off excess. Place ducks in hot oil and brown lightly on all sides. Remove duck from pot and set aside. Add onions, celery, bell peppers and minced garlic and sauté 5 to 7 minutes or until golden brown. Add tomatoes, RO*TEL®, tomato purée, stock, wine and thyme, scraping the bottom of pot to release browned bits. Return duck to pot and add mushrooms. Cover and bake for 3 hours or until meat is tender. Remove from oven and gently stir in parsley and green onions. Cover and let rest for 10 minutes. Adjust seasonings with salt, pepper and granulated garlic if necessary. Serve hot over steamed white rice or grits and garnish with parsley.

Donald Link with Chef John Folse, an extra treat for all

"To me it feels like a safe place, a place where I belong."
(l to r) Richard Zuschlag, Kim Bourriaque and Donald Link

Cajun frogging, purist style: Mac Dupuis

Cousins Blair Zuschlag and Mac Dupuis
treat us to a midnight frogging adventure.

JOHN CURRENCE

WITH VERA WILLIAMS
AT MALLARD REST

Mallard Rest: 5,800 acres of prime and prolific duck hunting.

VERA WILLIAMS CUTS AN IMPOSING FIGURE for a diminutive, 60-something Delta woman. She wears the look of someone who has fought for more sunrises than she ever thought of enjoying. She speaks softly but with authority. People listen intently when she talks and stand straighter than they normally would when in her presence. In Webb, Mississippi, a town ravaged by changes in traditional agricultural practices and peopled heavily by those who lurk in the shadows come sundown, she is respected – and obeyed. ¶ A block of fallen-in, burned-out and closed-down storefronts separates the Webb Diner from the next functioning business. Locals goof and backslap down the street, but at Ms. Vera's, it's all business. Locals and duck hunters alike file in as if they are going to dinner at their grandmother's house. Perhaps it's the Saturday Night Special strapped to her hip, but I like to believe sometimes folks just know when to act right.

THERE ISN'T A COOKBOOK in the place. Vera doesn't need any. She makes the 30-or-so minute ride to the closest grocery store to buy her ingredients each day. She doesn't buy from the big truck delivery services. She doesn't trust them. Vera prefers instead to touch her vegetables, poke her meats and smell her fish before she buys them. She cooks the way folks ought to cook: carefully selecting her ingredients individually and blending and cooking them from memory, from the heart. It shows in the finished product and in the response to what she does both at the Webb Diner and at Tommie and Billy Dunavant's Mallard Rest hunting club, where she moonlights during duck season.

Mr. Billy is not easily impressed. He doesn't have to be; he has built an empire on cotton. He is one of the country's most respected in his business and has assembled a refuge for duck hunting that anyone would envy equally.

The closest hunting field to the house is a six-year-old's stone's throw from the front porch. As I pull up, 25,000 to 30,000 ducks and geese light from that field. I am slack-jawed and almost run into the side of my host's car, amazed at the sight. Precisely one heavy pour of bourbon later, Mr. Billy is tearing through muddy cotton fields in a Suburban that has seen thousands of this sort of hours of wear and tear. The fields are no-till, thankfully, though I am certain that would not slow him down a bit. Billy blows by field after pond after slough after swamp hole, each erupting with another flurry of waterfowl.

I've never seen anything like it. To Billy, this is his birthright. The birds don't excite him the way they do me; the beauty of what he has created here does. Mallard Rest is as much his refuge as it is the ducks'.

For a man as well-heeled as Mr. Billy, Mallard Rest is understated. While many duck camps these days are built to astonish and are outfitted with absurdly expensive and overbuilt facilities, Mallard Rest is a model of functionality. It is neatly appointed with a smattering of trophies,

MALLARD REST

MALLARD REST is the Webb, Mississippi, duck hunting retreat for Billy Dunavant's closest friends and family. An invitation to Mallard Rest is highly coveted, and the property is renowned for its prolific duck hunting on 5,800 acres. The clubhouse is cozy and rustic, with four bedrooms. Its size makes it more suited to no-frills hunting trips rather than lavish entertaining, although Vera Williams and her cooking make Mallard Rest feel homey and comforting to all who stay there.

JOHN CURRENCE

JOHN CURRENCE was born and raised in New Orleans, where he worked his way up at several restaurants before settling in Oxford, Mississippi, in 1992 and opening City Grocery. In the time since, the City Grocery Restaurant Group has seen a number of openings, including Nacho Mama's, Kalo's, Ajax Diner, City Grocery Catering Company, Bouré, Big Bad Breakfast and Snackbar. Currence was recipient of both Restaurateur of the Year and Chef of the Year awards from the Mississippi Restaurant Association in 1998. He received the 2006 Southern Foodways Alliance Guardian of Tradition Award and won the 2008 Great American Seafood Cookoff in New Orleans. In 2009, he won the James Beard Award for Best Chef: South and was a winner of the Charleston Food and Wine Festival's Iron Chef Challenge.

VERA WILLIAMS

VERA WILLIAMS has been the owner and operator of the Webb Diner in Webb, Mississippi, since 1988 and has been catering at Mallard Rest since 1996. At the Webb Diner, she serves all customers, "from the desperately poor to the well-to-do," a clientele that runs the gamut from owners of big plantations and their field workers to Tallahatchie School District administrators to locals like Representative Benny Thompson and actor Morgan Freeman. Vera grew up in a family of 14 siblings in Tallahatchie County, learning to cook from her mother. She began her cooking career in a private home in the 1960s, and her talent in the kitchen served her in good stead raising nine children.

"She's a magician, and somehow I've just been fed one of the most enjoyable meals of my life." John Currence and Vera Williams

pictures of family and friends, a warm and welcoming great room anchored on either end by a cozy fireplace and a magnificent bar. Mallard Rest is perfect – it has exactly what a man would want or need before and after the hunt, but certainly isn't designed to pamper the prissy or squeamish. It is, quite simply, Billy Dunavant in a nutshell.

Vera Williams fits the Mallard Rest model perfectly. Whether she is cooking for the "Archduke of Cotton" or Webb's Main Street miscreants makes not a particle of difference to her. She deftly floats around the kitchen adding a pinch of this, a dash of that and a splash or two from a bottle of her homemade Sport Sauce. She stands confidently, arms crossed and leaning against her oven, watching an evening's whiskey-doused frenzy unfold. She is unfazed by anything she sees or hears. She chuckles from time to time, as likely from an awkward discomfort as from actual amusement. Vera Williams never stops working, even when her hands aren't moving.

We collapse, eventually, at the dining room table after a long afternoon of riding, storytelling and alcohol-fueled badinage. Food appears magically from every direction, and a hush blankets the boozy cacophony. Chicken and dumplings, pinto beans, turnips greens, mashed potatoes and gravy, pork chops and country-fried steak, each executed flawlessly, suggest a simpler time when everything was done with more care and, seemingly, less effort. In retrospect, it doesn't appear that Ms. Vera has raised a

finger. She's a magician, and somehow I've just been fed one of the most enjoyable meals of my life.

Our company slowly works its way from stunned silence back to the roar that had been momentarily tamed. Vera calmly emerges from the kitchen. She blushes gently at the attention and appreciates her bosses' affection. She and Billy Dunavant inhabit the same world in this moment, and I can spot a twinkle of pride in her eye as she unravels from his grasp.

Vera will pack her pots and pans and return them to the quiet corner that is the Webb Diner like she does several nights a week during duck season. For her it's just another night; for me it's a night I'll never forget. I've made new friends, passed a good time and watched a man not seemingly prone to gross sentimentality moved by a simple craft for the same reasons he is moved by the austere beauty of his little sanctuary. ❀

Talking shop in the diner: John Currence and Vera Williams

Vera's famous pepper sauce, dubbed Sport Sauce by John Currence

PORK CHOPS

VERA WILLIAMS

SERVES 4

I worked in a garment factory from 1965 to 1988, which was low-paying and not very satisfying. I'd always cooked. I had six brothers and seven sisters and raised nine children, and I just liked to cook for them. A lady from the factory said she wanted to sell her restaurant and asked me if I wanted to buy it. I said yes. I go in between 6:30 and 7:00 a.m., cook breakfast and stay until after lunch. We cook pork chops every Tuesday. This is something I just came up with on my own. My helpers do it at the diner, but I cook these pork chops at Mallard Rest.

- 4 BONE-IN, THIN-CUT PORK CHOPS
- SALT & BLACK PEPPER
- 2 EGGS
- ¼ CUP MILK
- VEGETABLE OIL FOR FRYING
- 2 CUPS ALL-PURPOSE FLOUR (SEASONED LIGHTLY WITH SALT, PEPPER & PAPRIKA)
- 2 CUPS SEASONED BREAD CRUMBS

RINSE AND PAT DRY pork chops. Season them with salt and black pepper and let stand at room temperature for 30 minutes. Lightly beat eggs and mix with milk. Heat 1 inch of vegetable oil in a skillet to 350 degrees. Dredge pork chops in flour and knock off any excess. Dip chops in egg mixture and then dip in bread crumbs. Place chops in oil and brown on each side for 3 minutes. Remove from oil and pierce with a fork. Chops should be firm and juices should be clear.

SINCE 1927

Blackburn-Made SYRUP

NET 40 FL. OZ. (1 QT. 8 OZ.) 1.183 L

Nutrition Facts
Serving Size 1/4 Cup 80 ml
Servings Per Container 14

Amount Per Serving

Calories 260

Total Fat 0g
Sodium 50mg
Total Carbohydrate 65g
  Sugars 38g
Protein 0g

*Percent Daily Values are based on
counts the

INGREDIENTS: CORN SYRUP, HIGH FRUCTOSE
CORN SYRUP, CANE SYRUP, WATER,
COLORING, SORBIC ACID, SODIUM
BENZOATE (ADDED AS A PRESERVATIVE)

T.J. BLACKBURN SYRUP WORKS, INC.
JEFFERSON, TX 75657 USA

SPORT SAUCE

VERA WILLIAMS

MAKES APPROXIMATELY 6 CUPS

NOTES:

Sport Sauce will keep chilled for months, and it is delicious on all types of greens and peas.

- 4 CUPS WHITE WINE VINEGAR
- 4 CUPS LITTLE SUMMER GARDEN PEPPERS (OR ANY COMBINATION OF SERRANO, BANANA, CAYENNE OR JALAPEÑO CHILE PEPPERS)
- ½ CUP SUGAR

PLACE VINEGAR, peppers and sugar in a pot and bring to a boil. Once pot comes to a boil, remove from heat. Allow mixture to cool completely. Divide into glass jars and refrigerate for 1 week before using.

CHICKEN AND DUMPLINGS

VERA WILLIAMS

SERVES 8

Billy Dunavant had a crew working for him who would come into the diner to eat. The manager told Mr. Dunavant about me and suggested I come in and cook at Mallard Rest. I hardly ever make chicken and dumplings at the diner, but I make it for them a lot at the hunting club. During duck hunting season, I go out there and do dinner in the evenings. I cook whatever they want, like meatloaf or chicken. I make it at my place and bring it already fixed, ready to eat.

CHICKEN:

- 1 CHICKEN (APPROXIMATELY 4 POUNDS)
- SALT & BLACK PEPPER
- 1 YELLOW ONION, QUARTERED
- 1 CARROT, CHOPPED
- 2 STALKS CELERY, CHOPPED
- 1 BAY LEAF
- 1 TABLESPOON SALT

RINSE CHICKEN, pat dry and season inside and out with salt and black pepper. Allow to stand at room temperature for 30 minutes. Place chicken, vegetables and salt in a deep pot and add enough water to cover by 2 inches. Bring to a boil and simmer for approximately 1 hour or until chicken is tender and falling apart. Allow to cool, remove chicken, strain vegetables and reserve liquid.

When chicken has cooled enough to handle, pull meat from bones and chop roughly.

DUMPLINGS:

- 3 TABLESPOONS SHORTENING
- 2 CUPS SELF-RISING FLOUR, PLUS EXTRA FOR ROLLING
- ½ CUP WARM MILK

IN A MIXING BOWL, cut shortening into flour with a fork. Stir in milk and blend until dough comes together. Remove to a floured surface and knead until smooth. Add flour if needed to make dough easier to handle. Roll dough ¼ inch thick and cut into ¾ inch squares. Dust squares with flour and set aside.

ASSEMBLY:

PLACE SHREDDED chicken in a pot, cover well with reserved stock and bring to a boil. Reduce to a simmer and add dumplings. Simmer until dumplings are plump and tender. Season to taste with salt and pepper.

"As I pull up, 25,000 to 30,000 ducks and geese light from that field. I am slack-jawed and almost run into the side of my host's car, amazed at the sight."

John Currence and Billy Dunavant

When they were just beginning to date, Billy Dunavant made his wife, Tommie, one of his specialties, fireplace duck. The recipe involves taking a duck, buttering and seasoning it and wrapping it in aluminum foil. The tightly-wrapped package goes straight into the hot embers of the fireplace. Fourteen minutes later, the foil is pulled back to reveal pink, succulent, perfectly cooked duck.

John Currence is rendered speechless – an unusual occurrence – upon the presentation of the perfect, 14-minute fireplace duck.

John T. Gaston, conservation and hunting manager of Mallard Rest, tends the fireplace duck.

ANDOUILLE PIGS IN A BLANKET

JOHN CURRENCE

MAKES APPROXIMATELY 3 DOZEN

BLANKET DOUGH:

- 2 CUPS SELF-RISING FLOUR, PLUS EXTRA FOR ROLLING
- 2 TEASPOONS SUGAR
- 3 TABLESPOONS LARD OR SHORTENING, CHILLED
- 3 TABLESPOONS BUTTER, CHILLED
- 1 CUP BUTTERMILK

WHISK TOGETHER flour and sugar in a bowl and cut lard or shortening and butter into flour with a fork until mix resembles coarse meal. Blend in buttermilk with a fork until dough comes together. Remove dough to a lightly-floured surface and knead until smooth. Roll dough ⅜ inch thick, and cut into 2 inch squares. Cut each square diagonally into two triangles.

ASSEMBLEY:

- ½ POUND ANDOUILLE SAUSAGE
- 1 EGG, LIGHTLY BEATEN

PREHEAT OVEN to 400 degrees. Cut sausage into 1 inch pieces and then quarter each piece lengthwise. Place sausage pieces at the wide end of dough triangles and roll up together. Seal pointed end of dough with egg. Brush tops with egg and bake for 12 minutes or until golden brown.

MOM'S DUCK AND MUSHROOM STEW

JOHN CURRENCE

SERVES 12

I ate a LOT of freezer-burned duck as a kid. I ate a lot of freezer-burned everything, for that matter. It's just the way it worked when I was little. Freezers were crappy, freezer bags were crappy and the end products that came from those things were typically crappy. My mom used to make this recipe that never failed to elevate those flavors. Plus it has the added appeal of the textural crunch of the water chestnuts, which is unusual and certainly not local to south Louisiana. It's one of those things that takes me back to a very good place – a place I knew my duck wasn't going to taste like the bottom of the freezer.

- 4 MALLARDS OR GREY DUCKS
- 2 YELLOW ONIONS, DICED
- 4 CARROTS, PEELED & DICED
- 5 STALKS CELERY, DICED
- 3 BAY LEAVES
- 2 TABLESPOONS FRESH THYME
- 1 TABLESPOON RED PEPPER FLAKES
- 4 CUPS RED WINE

COMBINE ALL ingredients in a pot and bring to a boil. Allow to simmer for 1½ hours or until duck is falling apart. Skim foam off of the surface as needed. Remove ducks, strain and reserve liquid. Pick duck meat and discard bones and vegetables.

- ½ CUP BUTTER
- ½ CUP FLOUR
- 2 YELLOW ONIONS, DICED
- 5 STALKS CELERY, DICED
- 3 GREEN BELL PEPPERS, DICED
- 3 TABLESPOONS GARLIC, MINCED
- 5 CUPS MUSHROOMS, SLICED
- 5 DRIED BAY LEAVES
- 2 TABLESPOONS DRIED TARRAGON
- 1 TABLESPOON DRIED BASIL
- 1 TABLESPOON DRIED THYME
- 3 CUPS RED WINE
- RESERVED DUCK COOKING LIQUID PLUS 6 CUPS DUCK STOCK
- 1½ TABLESPOONS TABASCO®
- 4 CUPS WATER CHESTNUTS, SLICED
- SALT & PEPPER TO TASTE
- 3 CUPS GREEN ONIONS, CHOPPED

MELT BUTTER in a very large pot and whisk in flour to make a roux. Whisk over low heat until the roux is deep brown. Stir in onions, celery, bell peppers, garlic and mushrooms and cook until softened. Add dry herbs, duck meat, red wine, reserved duck liquid and about 4 cups stock. Bring to a simmer.

Allow to cook for 25 to 30 minutes, adding more stock as needed. Remove bay leaves. Stir in Tabasco® and water chestnuts and season with salt and pepper.

At service, stir in green onions and serve over rice.

Billy Dunavant, the consummate host

John Currence and guest Frank Mitchner, longtime friend and
Mallard Rest neighbor from Sumner, Mississippi

"For her it's just another night; for me it's a night I'll never forget."

A club for close friends: Judith Mitchner and Tommie Dunavant

Tommie Dunavant says, "I love my Vera because she takes care of my Billy."

"Mallard Rest is perfect – it has exactly what a man would want or need before and after the hunt."

Mallard Rest is famous for its special house drink and "aiming oil," Sweet Lucy. As Tommie Dunavant says, "I may be the maker of Sweet Lucy, but I am not the inventor. I inherited the tradition of Sweet Lucy when I married Billy. He first began drinking this magical concoction when he and his friend Henry Morgan were goose hunting in Canada in the 1970s. On cold Canadian morning hunts, they would drink a 100-proof, honey-based Canadian whiskey 'to keep warm,' or so they said. Because it was so sweet, they tired of it quickly and decided to make their own brand of warming oil with Old Charter® bourbon and peach brandy. The original recipe was not complicated – simply ⅔ Old Charter® and ⅓ peach brandy. The name Sweet Lucy stuck.

"Over the years, I've evolved the recipe somewhat. Old Charter® and peach brandy are still the ingredients, with an added touch. As I began making batches of Sweet Lucy, I would decant some from each batch and age the drink.

"So today, the mix is ½ Old Charter®, ¼ peach brandy and ¼ aged Sweet Lucy. Whatever the mix, it is a necessity in the blind, where even preachers have been known to partake. Does it really help one aim and stay warm? Only the drinkers know. But one thing is for sure – without it, there would be fewer stories to tell.

"As Billy heads out to the hunt, one can always hear him yell back, 'Don't forget Sweet Lucy!'"

"Mallard Rest is as much his refuge as it is the ducks.'"

John Currence and Billy Dunavant take aim.

Simba does his job.

"To Billy, this is his birthright. The birds don't excite him the way they do me; the beauty of what he has created here does."

KELLY ENGLISH

WITH REBECCA SIMS
AT MENASHA

Setting the ground rules in Rebecca's kitchen:
Rebecca Sims and Kelly English

THE DIRECTIONS to Menasha read like many others: from the highway exit, wrap around to the service road, turn right at the largest telephone pole, cross the levee with the train tracks and follow the path until you see the camp. I'm sure I forgot about a fork in the road somewhere. That is where the similarities end between Menasha and all other camps trying to cast the shadows that this club does. This is not the converted school bus that I grew up hunting out of in Chipola, Louisiana, a little town on the banks of the Amite River in St. Helena Parish.

WHEN WE PULLED UP, club manager Roy Sims and his dog, Blinky (the only dog I have ever met that could tell the difference between a crappie and a bass) were at the boathouse getting gear together to fish. Roy brought us inside to meet his wife, Rebecca, the cook and housekeeper at Menasha.

The den at the club is inviting and comfortable, with large couches on which many a tale of the hunt has been shared. On the wall opposite the member log, which dates back to the 1970s, is a bulletin board made of corks from bottles most wine critics would kill to sip on. Walking through the dining room, it became quite obvious that meals here are taken seriously. Past the old farmhouse dining table and through the wall of windows was a living portrait of what a dining room view should be. I pulled myself away from the windows and went to get to know Rebecca.

Rebecca and I got to talking about what she does, how she cooks, her philosophy on food and her favorite things to eat. Rebecca's commitment to working out of a kitchen that makes her and the members proud is evident upon first stepping into the kitchen. Immediately I sensed the pride Rebecca takes in people enjoying her labors. She speaks in a very matter-of-fact tone about a certain dish until she mentions the name of the club member whose favorite it is, and then smiles widely. She knows the ingredients that each member favors and makes sure to keep them on hand, as evidenced by the stash of three different types of olive oil. Rebecca is quite particular, as any good chef is, about how she wants things prepared, as was apparent when I was "fired" for not flipping her famous corncakes correctly. These corncakes are the crown jewel of dinner for the members, specifically Menasha president Jim McGehee. Think about a hush puppy pretending to be a pancake, a generous spoonful of Montana honey on top, and you've got yourself a good time. The ones I had on my visit were so good, in fact, that we featured an homage to Rebecca and her corncakes the next week on the tasting menu at Restaurant Iris.

MENASHA HUNTING & FISHING CLUB

THOUGH THE ORIGINAL Menasha Hunting & Fishing Club near Turrell, Arkansas, was founded in 1902, the current clubhouse was built in 1974 and underwent an exhaustive renovation project in 2008. Menasha's 34 members take advantage of this 1,100-acre hunting and fishing paradise, where catching "20 to 30 bass a day is routine," according to club president Jim McGehee of Memphis. Members enjoy entertaining at the inviting clubhouse, which features 14 bedrooms. In the refurbishment of the club, the screen porch became a dining room with a wall of glass, maximizing the glorious view. Rebecca Sims, wife of Menasha manager Roy Sims, is on hand to cook for the members and guests at the club.

KELLY ENGLISH

KELLY ENGLISH is the executive chef and owner of Restaurant Iris in Memphis. His culinary style incorporates familiar flavors from his childhood in southern Louisiana into French-Creole cuisine. A graduate of the Culinary Institute of America, he spent several years training under John Besh in New Orleans before moving to Memphis to open Restaurant Iris. In 2009, Kelly celebrated the restaurant's first anniversary by being named one of *Food & Wine*'s "Best New Chefs." He was also a 2010 James Beard Award nominee for Best Chef: Southeast.

REBECCA SIMS

REBECCA SIMS has lived at Menasha and served as cook and housekeeper for its members and guests since 2003. Having learned to cook at age 12, Rebecca's prior professional experience was as proprietor of The Eat Shop in Harlowton, Montana, from 2000 to 2002. Before that, she had been a homemaker, substitute teacher, retailer and real estate agent. She and her husband, Roy, who ran farming and ranch operations for Dunavant Enterprises for 35 years, lived in more than a dozen towns in eight states before settling at Menasha. "I have recipes from everywhere we've lived," says Rebecca.

Rebecca Sims with Mary Robinson, wife of club member Bert Robinson

Kelly English with club president Jim McGehee

Kelly prepares his signature "salad" of Brussels sprouts, bacon and sherry, a first for
Menasha. (l to r) Gracie Mister, Rebecca Sims and Kelly English

The menu for supper that night will forever be one of the most unexpectedly inspiring dinners that I have been lucky enough to attend. People hear a lot about local foods, but when you eat at Menasha, you eat food that comes from within a half-mile radius of the club. Roy either grows every vegetable or Rebecca trades her home-grown produce with a neighbor to cook dinner. She makes jams once a year when the seasons are at their peak for the different fruits. The crappie, or sac-au-lait as I grew up calling it in Louisiana, were caught 20 paces east of the kitchen. The corn was grown on property, as was almost everything else on the table that night. Chefs across the country are lauded and given awards for sourcing locally and supporting sustainable agriculture, and we are passionate about it. For Rebecca and Roy, this has been a way of life more than a movement.

Fishing at Menasha is an absolutely surreal event. I walked down to the boathouse and was handed a rod and reel, the reel being quite superfluous for this occasion. Roy said all we needed to do was to drop the line in the water about five feet, give it a wiggle and yank up on the bite. I looked around and saw the club members who would be joining us for dinner that evening already had lines dropped, and I followed suit. I have never seen anything like what happened next. I didn't keep track of time, but I would venture to say we fished for 45 minutes to an hour. In that time period, we, as a group, caught at least six, five-gallon buckets full of crappie. I mentioned earlier that Blinky the dog knew the difference between crappie (for people to eat) and bass (for him). Blinky would run to the person who caught a bass and sit until it was given to him. From there, he would retreat into one of the members' boats and have his fill.

After we caught what I can only assume was everything in the county, I hopped into the fish cleaning house, a pontoon boat affixed to a pier. Roy was steady at work filleting the catch with a precision I had yet to see with an electric fillet knife – three smooth moves and the fish was ready for Rebecca. We brought the crappie back up to the

"All of the highfalutin dishes at my restaurant are ones that somehow remind our friends and guests about the type of food Rebecca serves. There is no better type of food than the simple dishes that make your eyes open a little, then close with a head shake."

kitchen, and Rebecca started seasoning and dredging. The crappie was both fried and sautéed in olive oil. The corn, creamed when it is in season, is frozen for use year-round. The slaw was made from cabbage grown around the corner. The property-grown butter beans rivaled my late grandmother's. My only regret is we were not there during tomato season; I would love to see the pride Rebecca takes in a tomato she and Roy grow.

Fancy dinners at Menasha are served in a very civilized buffet style, and the table was set for 16 guests. After everyone was seated, Jim McGehee presided over grace and thanks. The dinner wrapped up with many toasts. There was one to the fish, one to the guests and one to the camp. The most important one was for Rebecca, and that one ended with a standing ovation. Chefs like Rebecca are important to me; all of the highfalutin dishes at my restaurant are ones that somehow remind our friends and guests about the type of food she serves. There is no better type of food than the simple dishes that make your eyes open a little, then close with a head shake.

After dinner, I looked out over the water and surrounding flora, which has remained relatively unchanged since the camp was founded. The experience of this wonderful dinner with ingredients that came from the surrounding land and the commitment the members have to the camp and to each other brought everything back home for me. These men and women are, in every sense of the word, conservationists – of the camp, of the land and of a specific way of life. At Menasha they insist all regulations, both legal and ethical, are followed. They preserve the land, ensuring the grounds and waters are treated with the highest respect. They ascribe to a way of life that many people have forgotten, and that many people work very hard to recapture.

I will never forget spending the day at Menasha, cooking the bounty of the property with Rebecca. I can imagine her harvesting the gardens at Menasha, thinking about which member's favorite dish she just plucked from the soil and smiling broadly. Now I just have to figure out how to get invited back. ❁

Menasha president Jim McGehee signed the guest book that, through thousands of entries, records the club history for nearly 40 years. Jim was the first to sign the book in 1974, justifying his catch record of zero bass, bream or crappie with the note, "Just came for dinner & to show the club to in-laws & friends." His entry from August 26, 2003, reads: "To meet Roy & Rebecca & say farewell & thanks to [predecessors] Earl & Evelyn."

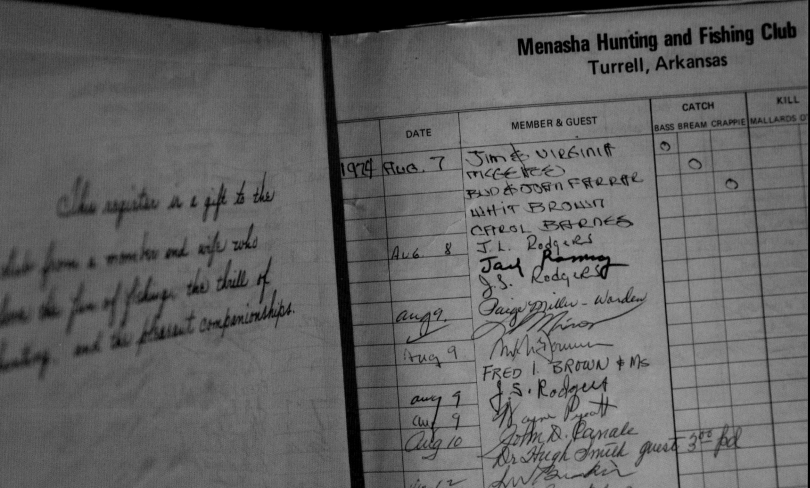

This register is a gift to the
club from a member and wife who
share the fun of fishing, the thrill of
hunting, and the pleasant companionships.

Menasha Hunting and Fishing Club
Turrell, Arkansas

DATE	MEMBER & GUEST	CATCH			KILL	
		BASS	BREAM	CRAPPIE	MALLARDS	
1974 Aug. 7	JIM & VIRGINIA McGEHEE	O				
	BUD & JOAN FARRAR		O			
	WHIT BROWN			O		
	CAROL BARNES					
Aug. 8	J. L. Rodgers					
	Jack Ramsey					
	J. S. Rodgers					
aug 9	Paige Miller - Warden					
Aug 9						
	FRED I. BROWN & Ms					
aug 9	J. S. Rodgers					
aug 9	Wayne Pyeatt					
Aug 10	John D. Canale					
	Dr. Hugh Smith guest 3⁰⁰ pd					
aug 12						

Fishing at Menasha, a surreal event: "I have never seen anything like [it]."
(l to r) Blinky, Kelly English and club member Bert Robinson

"After we caught what I can only assume was everything in the county…": Kelly English weighs in.

Roy Sims prepares the catch "with a precision I had yet to see with an electric fillet knife – three smooth moves and the fish was ready for Rebecca."

The fish cleaning house, a pontoon affixed to a pier

MY FATHER'S GRILLADES

KELLY ENGLISH

SERVES 4

I remember eating these grillades every Sunday growing up (whether that is the truth or just an overactive memory is really of no consequence). My father has always been a great cook, and this was a recipe he taught me when I was in high school. The great part about his recipe is that it was never written; it was truly passed down. I can only hope he will forgive me for putting it in print, which should not be much of an issue if he reads this after a successful hunt.

- 1 POUND PORK LOIN, CLEANED OF ALL FAT AND SILVER SKIN
- KOSHER SALT
- FRESHLY GROUND BLACK PEPPER
- SALT-FREE CREOLE OR CAJUN SEASONING (I LIKE KONRIKO®)
- 2 CUPS FLOUR
- ½ CUP CANOLA OIL
- ½ CUP BUTTER
- 1 ONION, FINELY CHOPPED
- 1½ STALKS CELERY, FINELY CHOPPED
- 1 GREEN BELL PEPPER, FINELY CHOPPED
- 1 TABLESPOON GARLIC, MINCED
- 1 WHOLE TOMATO, DICED (CANNED IF TOMATOES ARE NOT IN SEASON)
- 1 TABLESPOON FRESH THYME, CHOPPED
- 1 QUART BEEF STOCK (IF NOT HOMEMADE, USE ORGANIC & LOW SODIUM)
- 1 BAY LEAF
- 1 TABLESPOON WORCESTERSHIRE SAUCE

PREHEAT OVEN to 250 degrees. Slice pork loin into ¼ inch medallions. Place each medallion between two pieces of waxed paper and pound evenly and gently until very thin. Vigorously season medallions with kosher salt, freshly ground black pepper and Cajun or Creole seasoning on both sides. Lightly season the flour with the same three seasonings, and dredge pork medallions in the flour mixture. Heat canola oil in a large, heavy-bottomed pot over high heat. Dip the corner of one of the dredged pork medallions in oil. If it begins to fry, then the oil is ready. If it doesn't fry, wait until oil is hot enough (375 degrees). When oil is ready, sear all of the pork (on both sides) in the oil. Place all of the seared pork on a plate to rest, and set aside. Drain all but 2 tablespoons of the oil out of the pan and turn the heat down to medium low. Add the butter to the pot, and once melted, stir in leftover seasoned flour from the dredging. Slowly cook the roux (this could take 45 minutes), stirring every minute or two with a wooden spoon, scraping all of the edges. Never walk away from the pot. Once roux has taken on the color of semi-dark chocolate, add onion, celery and bell pepper (collectively known as the "trinity" in Cajun cooking). Cook your trinity until it has softened. Add garlic, tomato and thyme. Cook for a minute or until you can smell the garlic. Whisk in stock and add bay leaf and Worcestershire sauce. Season with salt, pepper and Creole seasoning. Bring to a simmer and add seared pork back to the pot. Cover the pot with foil and place in the oven for 1 to 1½ hours. Remove bay leaf. Serve over your favorite stone ground grits and top with poached eggs.

MENASHA CORNCAKES

REBECCA SIMS

SERVES 8

When I came to Menasha, I was told I had to serve corncakes with pear preserves at every meal. The lady who worked at Menasha before me would just make cornbread, cut it and fry it. I'd been making Roy hot water cornbread, and I combined it with a recipe from *Southern Living*. The members at Menasha love it with my pear preserves – that is the tradition at the club. When I came to the club in 2003, I brought some Montana honey with me. I introduced that honey, which Jim McGehee, Chip Dudley and some other members love on the corncakes.

- 2 CUPS SELF-RISING CORNMEAL (I LIKE AUNT JEMIMA®)
- ¼ CUP HALF & HALF
- 1 TABLESPOON OLIVE OIL
- 1¼ CUP BOILING WATER
- CANOLA OIL FOR COOKING

WHISK TOGETHER cornmeal, half and half and olive oil and add enough boiling water until you reach the consistency of cooked grits. Cover the bottom of a medium heavy skillet with canola oil and heat over high heat to approximately 375 degrees. Ladle the batter by heaping ¼ cupfuls into the oil. Do not ladle more than four or five at a time. Flatten cakes with the back of the spoon and cook until golden brown, approximately 2 to 3 minutes per side.

PEAR PRESERVES

REBECCA SIMS

YIELDS APPROXIMATELY 4 CUPS

- 8 CUPS PEARS, CORED, PEELED & THINLY SLICED
- 4 CUPS SUGAR
- 1 LEMON, THINLY SLICED

MIX ALL ingredients in a large pot and let sit covered overnight or 8 to 10 hours. Sterilize jars and lids in boiling water at least 10 minutes. Let simmer while making jam. Bring mixture to a rapid boil and stir constantly until mixture is slightly thickened and fruit is translucent and a rich amber/tan color. Pour jam quickly into hot, sterilized jars. Make sure rims are completely clean before topping with lids. Process jars in boiling water for 10 minutes to seal. Place in a draft-free area covered with a dish towel until cooled and lids have popped.

Corncakes, the crown jewel of dinner: "Think about a hush puppy pretending to be a pancake."

"SALAD" OF BRUSSELS SPROUTS, BACON & SHERRY

KELLY ENGLISH

SERVES 4

Brussels sprouts have always reminded me of the place where I grew up, southern Louisiana. In fact, Louisiana was the first place in North America to grow these little treats after the French settlers brought them over. They are understated, have so much character and are absolutely delicious. If you don't treat them right, though, you will hate them forever (overcooking is the main reason that they are so vilified). There really is nothing more satisfying than eating the bounty of your childhood soil with a roasted duck that you hunted.

- 40 BRUSSELS SPROUTS, TRIMMED
- 2 TABLESPOONS SHERRY VINEGAR
- ⅓ CUP OLIVE OIL
- 8 BENTON'S SMOKED COUNTRY BACON OR OTHER THICK-CUT BACON SLICES, CUT INTO SHORT STRIPS
- 2 SHALLOTS, MINCED
- 4 GARLIC CLOVES, MINCED
- 3 TABLESPOONS FRESH THYME, CHOPPED
- SALT & PEPPER TO TASTE

CUT BRUSSELS SPROUTS in half, lengthwise. Blanch in 1 gallon of boiling water seasoned generously with salt until sprouts are tender but not mushy. Remove immediately and place in a large bowl of ice water to shock. Pat sprouts dry and set aside. Whisk together vinegar and olive oil in a small bowl and set aside. Render the strips of bacon in a large sauté pan over medium heat. When bacon begins to brown and crisp, add sprouts. Once sprouts start to take on some color, add shallots, garlic and thyme. When shallots become translucent, coat the salad (still in the pan) with sherry vinaigrette to taste and season with salt and freshly ground pepper. Enjoy!

Roy Sims grows all of the fruit and vegetables served at Menasha on the club's property. "Chefs across the country are lauded and given awards for sourcing locally and supporting sustainable agriculture, and we are passionate about it," says Kelly English. "For Rebecca and Roy, this has been a way of life more than a movement." Rebecca prepares the bounty of Roy's garden and "puts up" the produce to be stored and used year-round in different ways. She freezes corn, pickles okra and makes pear preserves, the traditional topping for her corncakes.

A whole new meaning to eating local: "When you eat at Menasha, you eat food that comes from within a half-mile radius of the club. Roy either grows every vegetable or Rebecca trades her home-grown produce with a neighbor." Club manager and Rebecca's husband, Roy Sims

"Rebecca is quite particular, as any good chef is, about how she wants things prepared, as was apparent when I was 'fired' for not flipping her famous corncakes correctly."

There are many toasts, one to the guests, one to the fish and one to the camp.
(l to r) Suzy Brown, Julie Johnson, Penny Keras, Jim McGehee, Mary Robinson and Jim Keras

SLAW

REBECCA SIMS

SERVES 6-8

I just created my own slaw with this recipe. I especially like the texture of the sunflower seeds, and I recommend finely shredding the cabbage.

NOTES:

To shred cabbage, place the cabbage on a cutting board and, with a large, sharp knife, cut in quarters lengthwise. Remove the core. Finely slice each cabbage quarter to create thin strands.

- ⅓-½ CUP MAYONNAISE
- 2 TEASPOONS WHITE WINE VINEGAR
- 2 TEASPOONS SUGAR
- SALT & PEPPER TO TASTE
- 1 BAG CABBAGE OR BROCCOLI SLAW MIX OR 4 CUPS SLICED CABBAGE & 2 GRATED CARROTS
- ½ CUP SUNFLOWER SEEDS
- ¼ CUP RED OR SWEET ONION, THINLY SLICED OR MINCED

WHISK TOGETHER mayonnaise, vinegar, sugar, salt and pepper. Combine well with remaining ingredients. Cover and refrigerate.

SPICY & SWEET STRAWBERRY "SALSA FRESCA"

KELLY ENGLISH

SERVES 4

Fishing in the spring and summer always brought my family together. My grandparents lived on the west fork of the Calcasieu River near Sulphur, Louisiana, and at least once a year we would all get together and fish. My grandmother was, in my opinion, the best cook ever to live, and it was her inspiration that brought along this "salsa fresca." Feel free to use whatever fruit or berry you like; it is wonderful during peach season as well.

- 1 JALAPEÑO PEPPER
- 16 STRAWBERRIES, HULLED
- 18 CILANTRO LEAVES
- 6 MINT LEAVES
- ¼ TEASPOON SAMBAL OELEK CHILI PASTE
- 2 TABLESPOONS SUGAR
- 1 LIME, ZESTED & JUICED
- ½ TABLESPOON RICE WINE VINEGAR
- SALT TO TASTE

GRILL OR BROIL jalapeño over high heat until the skin is blistered and blackened in spots. Place in a small bowl and cover with plastic wrap to steam for about 15 minutes. Once cooled, peel, seed and chop jalapeño. Mince strawberries and thinly slice or chiffonade cilantro and mint. Combine all ingredients in a bowl and let the salsa rest for an hour before serving.

NOTES:

Makes a perfect alternate topping for the corncakes on page 200.

Sambal oelek chili paste is an Indian pepper paste that can be found at specialty food stores.

CRAPPIE TWO WAYS

REBECCA SIMS

SERVES 3-4

Crappie is the fish of choice of Menasha. When I first started cooking crappie, I cooked the fillets the way I had learned to cook shrimp in St. Augustine, Florida. I used to deep-fat fry the fillets in the beginning. But then my husband had a heart stent put in, and we have some other heart patients who are members of the club, so I started pan-searing the fish in olive oil to be a little lighter, a little healthier.

NOTES:

A splatter screen really helps to contain the oil while frying.

The amount of salt needed for these recipes varies depending on how much salt is in your other seasonings. Be sure to check the labels on the back, and adjust as needed.

If cracker meal is not available for the deep fried crappie, then make your own by finely grinding saltine crackers.

DEEP FRIED CRAPPIE

- 8 CRAPPIE FILLETS
- ¾ CUP CRACKER MEAL
- ¾ CUP CORNMEAL (I LIKE AUNT JEMIMA®)
- 1 TABLESPOON SALT-FREE LEMON PEPPER
- 1 TABLESPOON LEMON & HERB SEASONING
- 1 TABLESPOON MORTON NATURE'S SEASONS® SEASONING BLEND
- SALT & PEPPER TO TASTE
- 2 EGGS, LIGHTLY BEATEN
- CANOLA OR OTHER OIL FOR FRYING

MIX TOGETHER cracker meal, cornmeal and all seasonings (including salt and pepper if needed) and place in a shallow bowl or dish. Place beaten eggs in a separate dish. Dip each fillet in the eggs, coating completely. Remove fish and coat well with seasoned breading.

Fill a heavy Dutch oven ⅓ full of canola oil, and heat oil until hot (approximately 350 degrees). Drop in breaded fillets 4 to 5 at a time and cook until golden brown. Place fillets on a paper towel-lined platter to absorb excess oil. Sprinkle lightly with salt if desired and serve immediately.

PAN FRIED CRAPPIE

- 8 CRAPPIE FILLETS
- 1½ TEASPOONS SALT-FREE LEMON PEPPER
- 1 TEASPOON LEMON AND HERB SEASONING
- 1½ TEASPOONS MORTON NATURE'S SEASONS® SEASONING BLEND
- SALT & PEPPER TO TASTE
- 3-4 TABLESPOONS OLIVE OIL FOR PAN FRYING

RINSE FILLETS and blot dry with paper towels. Place dried fillets on a clear plastic wrap-lined cookie sheet or plastic or glass tray. Sprinkle both sides of fillets with a mixture of salt-free lemon pepper, lemon and herb seasoning, Nature's Seasons®, salt and pepper.

Cover the bottom of a large non-stick fry pan with olive oil and heat over medium high heat. When hot, place 4 to 5 fillets in oil and cook until meat is almost white and edges are golden. Turn fish once to brown on the other side.

Menasha president Jim McGehee partners with his cousin Scott McGehee in Tuscany to produce Maghí extra virgin olive oil. Their facility near Arezzo cold-presses the olives from 300 local growers, bottles and labels the oil. Maghí's natural acidity allows the oil to achieve the high Italian standard to be certified extra virgin. While 90 percent of the olive oil is sold in Italy, it is available through distributors on the West Coast, in Little Rock and in Memphis, where it is served at some of the city's finest restaurants, including Kelly English's Restaurant Iris.

The original Menasha clubhouse, built in the early 1900s

KAREN CARRIER

WITH EMMA LINCOLN
AT QUAIL HOLLOW

An immediate connection: Emma Lincoln and Karen Carrier

MY FIRST ENCOUNTER with Emma Mayweather Lincoln was at the Memphis home of Tommie and Billy Dunavant. I was a guest at a gathering to introduce the concept of this fantastic book. As usual, I arrived late, not being able to find the driveway to the house. While I was making my way through the den, the wait staff was passing succulent nuggets that were so moist they melted in my mouth. I wasn't sure what they were but I knew I wanted more. I found myself meandering through the house until I found the kitchen. The heart of the matter is always in the kitchen: the belly of the beast, the conversation table.

AS I ENTERED the bustling kitchen, a woman standing strong with a Jamaican beret on her head turned to see who I was. I introduced myself while I was eyeing the platter of nuggets. Emma turned to me with her warm smile and informed me they were Mr. Dunavant's favorite appetizer, fried wild turkey nuggets served with a horseradish cream dipping sauce. These were wild turkeys shot by Billy and brought to Emma to prepare, just as he had done years prior when her mother, Beneva Mayweather, cooked for his family's parties.

Emma and I had an immediate connection. Her warm smile, strong hands, nurturing ways and attention to detail in the kitchen were all I needed to realize I was meeting a gem.

Emma, and Beneva before her, has been responsible for the daily lunch at Dunavant Enterprises for 30 years. The Dunavants' caterers of choice, Emma and Beneva for decades have cooked at their home in Memphis, at their Mississippi hunting lodges, one time even preparing a "Southern supper" in Portland, Maine. Before I left the kitchen, Tommie Dunavant put her arms around Emma and shared with me how much Emma means to her. It was so heartfelt that it almost brought me to tears. This was an extended family, and I realized very early on how lucky I was be asked to be a part of its history.

This leads me to my trip to Quail Hollow on December 30, 2009. Dana Baldwin, my catering partner, and I struck off around five o'clock in the morning. Upon arrival at the Quail Hollow sign, we meandered up the long driveway. One road led to a modern ranch-style abode and the other to an older lodge. We chose the route to the newer home, and I got out of my car and knocked on the door. From the front door windows I saw a roaring fire in the fireplace and a large flat-screen television in the living room tuned to the morning news, but my knocks went unanswered. I opened the door and quietly let myself in. Realizing no one was home, I walked outside around the back to a spectacular view of miles and miles of land on the edge of a lake. How comforting it felt out there in the early morning dew. I could hear the sounds of wild ducks and geese talking amongst themselves in the background, and the air was crisp and fresh.

QUAIL HOLLOW

SET ON 5,800 ACRES in the rolling hill country near Coffeeville, Mississippi, Quail Hollow is the duck and turkey hunting preserve of Memphis cotton merchant Billy Dunavant and his wife, Tommie. In addition to excellent hunting land and an 80-acre lake stocked with fish, the property includes two houses, one for the Dunavants and their friends and one for the children and grandchildren to stay in and entertain. While caretaker Wesley Ross is usually on hand to feed Quail Hollow guests, for 10 years cook Emma Lincoln (like her mother before her) has prepared the meals for special occasions including New Year's Eve and the annual Father and Son Hunt.

KAREN CARRIER

KAREN BLOCKMAN CARRIER returned from New York City to Memphis in 1987 and launched Another Roadside Attraction Catering. In 1991, she opened Automatic Slim's Tonga Club, a sibling to the original outpost in New York. Having sold Memphis' Automatic Slim's in 2008, Karen's eateries now include Beauty Shop Restaurant and Lounge, included in *Gourmet*'s "America's Top 100 Restaurants" in 2002 and *Condé Nast Traveler*'s "Hot Tables" of 2003; Sushi + Dō Noodles; Mollie Fontaine Lounge; and Noodle Doodle Do, which was listed in 2009 in *Bon Appetit*'s "Hot Ten Best New Asian Noodle Bars in America." Karen was invited to cook for the prestigious James Beard House in New York City in 2000 and again in 2006.

EMMA LINCOLN

EMMA LINCOLN is the owner of Emma Lincoln Catering, a full-service catering business in Memphis that serves "from two to 2,000." The catering business is a continuation of the company her mother, Beneva Mayweather, formed in 1973. Emma joined the business in the mid-1970s and worked alongside her mother, taking on more and more responsibility throughout the years. Prior to her career in catering, Emma graduated from the University of Tennessee and earned a master's of library science from the University of Memphis. She was a teacher for two and a half years before joining her mother's business and starting a family, which includes son Daniel Watson, who is marketing a mix of spices from Beneva's recipes, and daughter Rashana Lincoln, who works with Emma.

Mary Frances Ingram, "the hush puppy queen from down the road"; in the background, Emma Lincoln and Tommie Dunavant

As we doubled back and drove up the other driveway, we parked next to a white, dusty pickup with a fresh deer head coming out of a pail in the bed of the truck. I looked at Dana, and we both broke out in laughter. Oh yeah, we knew we were at the right hunting lodge. No flat screen here!

Upon entering, I was struck by the large kitchen straight out of the 1950s. Emma and her right-hand lady, Margaret Jackson, had arrived at Quail Hollow three days prior to cook for the weekend's festivities. In the kitchen were Emma with her black apron; Margaret; Wesley Ross, the keeper of the hunting lodge; and the Dunavants' two big Labrador retrievers. Wesley lives on the land, where he cleans the wild game of the day and assists Emma in the frying of catfish and chicken out on the back screened-in porch. How I love those screened-in porches! Being raised in the South during the 1950s and 1960s, our family memories were made on screened-in porches, like the one at my grandparents' house.

As I made my way around the kitchen, I noticed all of Emma's lists: for lunch, for dinner and of course for the New Year's Eve preparation. I eyed Emma's recipe book sitting on the sideboard right next to her caramel cake. Emma was starting to prepare wild duck quesadillas for passed appetizers at lunch. I asked how I could help, put on my apron and was ready to get down and dirty. I didn't come here to observe; I wanted to cook. When food is your core, your calling and your livelihood, there is no rest.

Smoked wild duck quesadillas; country ham boiled down in sugar, thick sliced and served with red eye gravy; thick sliced bacon brought in from Texas; black crowder peas raised on the land; wild savory quail; wild turkey breast cut into small nuggets soaked in buttermilk and fried; barbeque pork ribs; barbeque baked beans; fried catfish; fried chicken; potato salad; hush puppies; homemade peppermint ice cream with chocolate sauce; and Brandy Alexanders with Emma's homemade vanilla ice cream,

which could knock you naked if you had too many! Emma asked me to beat the duck to tenderize it for country fried duck, and I was ready. I noticed some beautiful wild pheasant breasts sitting in a bowl in the sink that were to be used later for pheasant pot pie. They had to be soaked overnight in salt water. My mouth was starting to water just smelling the aromas wafting in this kitchen.

The back door to the kitchen opened, and in walked Mary Frances Ingram, the hush puppy queen from down the road! No questions were asked; she went right to her place. You have to understand these morsels of cornmeal batter. If you fry them too fast, they are mushy on the inside and burnt on the outside. Emma turned to me and let me know she didn't have the patience for them. I understood completely. We looked for the small ice cream scoop in the kitchen drawer so Mary Frances could get on with her steady hand and the art of frying hush puppies. These morsels were absolutely the best I have ever put in my mouth. Emma made the batter, but Mary Frances finished the job to perfection. The best cooks I've known have also been the most beautiful to watch in action. I must have popped 10 hush puppies in my mouth within the course of five minutes! Mary Frances would look at me with a quiet, sweet smile of permission as if to say, "It's okay, child. Keep eating!"

As Emma was setting up the platters for the luncheon, the guests were arriving through the kitchen door. I understood then what a tradition this is, not only for Emma but for the

"I didn't come here to observe; I wanted to cook. When food is your core, your calling and your livelihood, there is no rest."

Dunavants and their guests. Everyone knew Emma and was so excited about eating the familiar bounty she was about to put on the buffet. Billy came into the kitchen smiling and hugging all the girls, cracking jokes while the wine was flowing. Tommie came in bearing gifts with her gracious Southern style, so excited we were all there to experience what she knew was a feast to behold.

As the guests went into the dining room that looks out over the fields and lake, platters of food were passed, Emma and I got a chance to exchange our war stories. As we talked, we realized how parallel our lives are based on our catering experiences. Emma was led into the food business kicking and screaming. It was a family affair. Her mother built a catering kitchen next door to their home in the early 1960s. Her grandmother would sew the aprons and clothes; her father would bartend and run the errands; and she and her sisters would help Beneva prep and run the parties. As Emma spoke of her mother, her eyes would sparkle. Emma's reference to her mother's passion for cooking was so evident in everything she would say and do: her attention to detail, being true to her art, having made a good living for her kids and wanting her children to find their own passions.

Emma and I both started out as teachers. She quit teaching to have her children, divorced and came full circle into her mother's world of catering. Nearly 40 years later, she's still at it. I left New York City in 1987 to return home to Memphis, marry, have a family and start my culinary journey in the South. I moved home from the City and starting catering out of our home, taking over the kitchen and dining room. I was what we called in New York a closet caterer, eventually turning the carriage house in the back into a commercial catering kitchen. When my first son, Travis, was only three months old, we would put him in the middle of a prep table in his small rocker. He would stare up at all the women surrounding him as we would chop, slice and prepare food on my dining room table, spinning him around and singing all the way. Travis would gaze up at us like we were crazy and break out into big smiles, as if he could tell we were engrossed and happy doing our work.

My two sons started prepping and working in the business when they were 13 years old. Emma's children did the same. With Emma divorced and my husband deceased, we were single moms who were enabled by the food business to give our kids a great education, travel with them and make sure they understood the purity of a good work ethic. The world of food has taught our children social skills, serving the public, interacting with others in a work environment and the ability to make a living.

Cooks find themselves immersed in their kitchens. Sometimes we discover that we are spending more time with our kitchen families than our own flesh and blood. This is the world of food most don't understand – the movement in the kitchens, the sweat, long hours, sore muscles, routine, personal history, imagination and inspiration. My inspiration comes from the people who work the line and share that common thread. Emma's inspiration came from her mother. This is the soul of cooking. I raise a toast to Emma Mayweather Lincoln, a true inspiration. This is a testament to all cooks who find inner joy in preparing and seeing the immediate gratification that their history, handed down from generation to generation, brings to the table. ❀

The annual New Year's tradition unfolds.

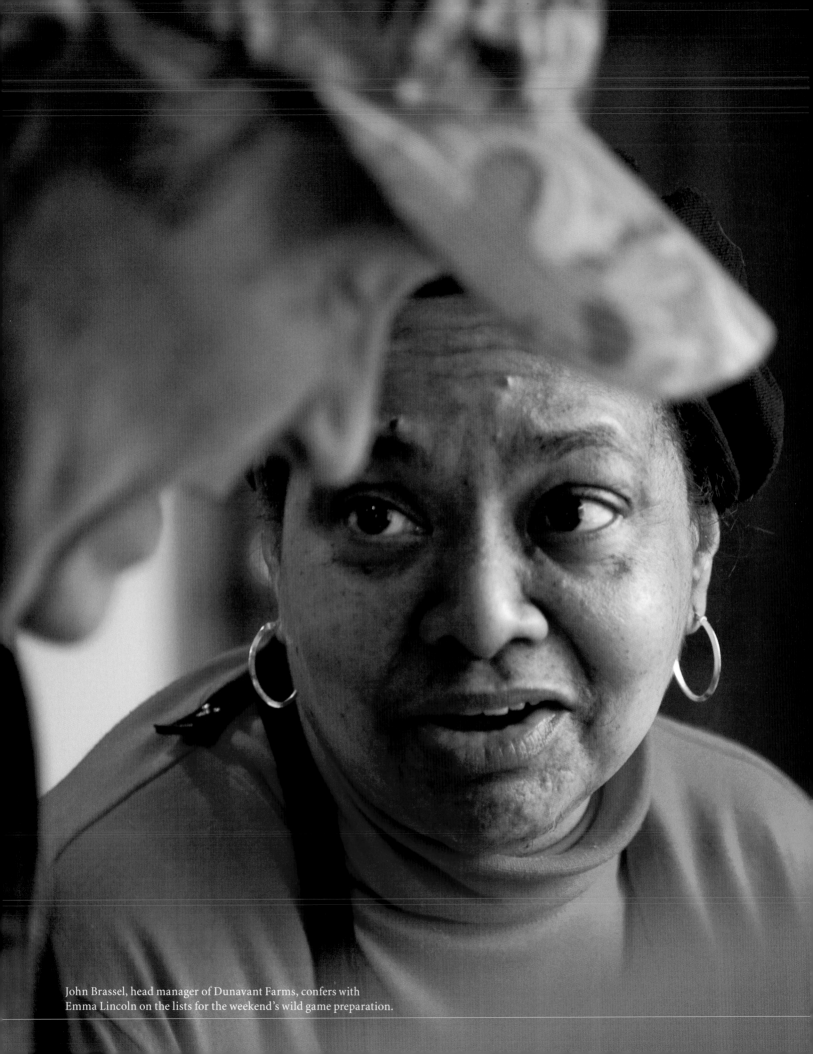

John Brassel, head manager of Dunavant Farms, confers with
Emma Lincoln on the lists for the weekend's wild game preparation.

Each year, Tommie and Billy Dunavant's New Year's Eve celebration ritual includes two days of hunting at their club Mallard Rest, in the Mississippi Delta, followed by two days at Quail Hollow. The club provides the perfect location for the coterie of friends to gather, enjoy the camaraderie in the blinds and around the table, reflect on the year past and share their hopes and expectations for the year ahead.

(l to r) Tommie Dunavant, Billy Dunavant and Emma Lincoln

The ritual and revelry: (clockwise from l) Haywood Smith, Alice Rawlins, Phil Burnett, Tommie Dunavant, Billy Dunavant and Layte Dopp

Old friends reunite: Haywood Smith and Emma Lincoln

CARIBBEAN CHICKEN STEW WITH JOHNNY CAKES

KAREN CARRIER

SERVES 4-6

As I was helping Emma prepare her pheasant pot pie, it brought back memories of my years in Jamaica learning how to cook on the beach with Ms. Winnie. These two women, though worlds apart, were so alike. Their kindness, fortitude and unwavering strength have left a lasting impression. There is a comfort and ease to these women – something I knew without question I wanted to be around.

Ms. Winnie has passed on but has left behind her legacy and knowledge of Jamaican cuisine not available in a restaurant or by reading a Caribbean cookbook. Most people would have called her a squatter; but to watch her schlep her pots, utensils, ingredients and seasonings onto the beach in Negril, I called her a saint. She was my food guru and my inspiration with her beautiful smile, petite frame and hands as strong as any fisherman or construction laborer.

With no kitchen to call her own, Ms. Winnie would dig a hole in the sand every morning and build a fire. Lunch was callaloo, crab and vegetable patties with lots of onions, thyme, allspice and scotch bonnet peppers in a silky, flaky coco flour dough, which she would lightly sauté in a skillet over some almond, allspice or hardwood branches. She'd make chicken foot soup with dumplings, fried chicken with her special spice blends, rice and peas in coconut milk and sautéed chayote in butter with chilies and fresh thyme. Grab a bottle of Pickapeppa® sauce, a cold Red Stripe® or an Appleton® rum and ting – what more could you want!

NOTES:

Most butchers will cut up the chicken for you, or you can buy separate pieces and cut the breasts in half.

- 1 WHOLE CHICKEN
- ¼ CUP OF OLIVE OIL TO COAT CHICKEN COMPLETELY
- 2 TEASPOONS GARLIC, MINCED
- SALT & PEPPER TO TASTE
- 1 TEASPOON NUTMEG
- 1 TEASPOON ALLSPICE
- ½ TEASPOON RED PEPPER FLAKES
- 3 TABLESPOONS OLIVE OIL FOR SEARING CHICKEN
- 2 TURNIPS, PEELED & CUT INTO 1½ INCH CHUNKS
- 2 BEETS, PEELED & CUT INTO 1½ INCH CHUNKS
- 2 LARGE CARROTS, PEELED & CUT INTO 1½ INCH CHUNKS
- 3 POTATOES, PEELED & CUT INTO 1½ INCH CHUNKS
- 1 SWEET POTATO, PEELED & CUT INTO 1½ INCH CHUNKS
- 2 TABLESPOONS GINGER, GRATED & SKIN LEFT ON
- 1 ONION, PEELED & CUT INTO EIGHTHS
- 1 CAN COCONUT MILK
- 1 CUP CHICKEN STOCK
- ZEST OF 2 LIMES OR LEMONS FOR GARNISH
- 2 TABLESPOONS CRYSTALLIZED GINGER, COARSELY CHOPPED FOR GARNISH

PREHEAT OVEN to 375 degrees. Cut chicken into thigh, drumstick and breast pieces, then cut each breast horizontally. You will have 8 pieces total. Drizzle chicken with the olive oil, garlic, salt, pepper, nutmeg, allspice and red pepper flakes. In a large roasting pan over medium high heat, add 3 to 4 tablespoons of olive oil and sear chicken in batches, turning occasionally until the skin is golden, approximately 6 minutes per batch. Add other ingredients through chicken stock and put the pan into the oven, covered, until thighs and legs are done, approximately 30 minutes. Remove from oven and transfer to a large bowl to serve. Garnish with lime or lemon zest and crystallized ginger. Serve with Johnny cakes.

JOHNNY CAKES

- 1 CUP CREAM-STYLE CORN
- 1 CUP CORNMEAL
- 2 EGGS, BEATEN
- ½ CUP VEGETABLE OIL
- 1 CUP MUENSTER CHEESE, GRATED
- 3 JALAPEÑO PEPPERS, MINCED
- 2 SCALLIONS, CHOPPED
- ½ CUP BUTTERMILK
- 1 TEASPOON BAKING SODA
- ½ TEASPOON SALT

GENTLY MIX all ingredients together. Heat an electric griddle or cast iron skillet on medium heat. Coat griddle or cast iron skillet with non-stick cooking spray or oil. Spoon batter by scant ¼ cupfuls onto the surface of griddle or skillet. Once tiny bubbles start forming on the top of the Johnny cakes, flip them over. They will cook like pancakes, about 1½ minutes on each side. Serve immediately.

CRISPY DUCK PIZZETTE

KAREN CARRIER

SERVES 4

Every Sunday my kosher, orthodox Jewish family would gather around the kitchen table to graze on corned beef, pastrami, tongue and beef fry sandwiches. This was a tradition in our house. No bacon, bologna, sausages, shrimp, oysters …you get the picture. Years later when I started art college I met some friends at Burkle's Bakery, an institution in Memphis in the 1950s through the mid-1970s. It was a bakery and a blue plate restaurant. A blue plate is a meat and three – you know, a fish or meat entrée and a list of Southern-style vegetables to choose from. Burkle's was a meeting place for all the hipsters and midtown families. When the waitress came to take our order, I asked her what catfish was. She stood back, looked me up and down, arched her painted-on eyebrow and said "Shug, you must not be from heyar?," and I said "Am too."

I told her I had never eaten catfish, shellfish or bacon in my life. She couldn't believe her ears and quickly asked "Watcha' momma fix u growin' up, sweetie?" Somehow I did not think she would understand the likes of matzo ball soup, latkes, beef fry or kugel, so I just went along with her and ordered my first taste of catfish with an extra side of bacon! I guess if you never had anything to compare beef fry to, one might not know that this substitute for bacon was truly sacrilegious! Once I had the real slab I never looked back.

NOTES:

Unagi (eel sauce) and Togarashi chile blend are available at Asian grocery stores.

Health officials note that raw eggs should not be consumed by young children, pregnant women, the elderly or anyone with a weakened immune system. To avoid the risk of salmonella, you can substitute pasteurized egg yolk in the aioli.

- 2 DUCK BREASTS (APPROXIMATELY 5 OUNCES EACH)
- 2 TABLESPOONS KOSHER SALT & BLACK PEPPER
- 1 TABLESPOON OLIVE OIL
- 5 SLICES BENTON'S SMOKED COUNTRY BACON OR OTHER GOOD QUALITY BACON
- 4 FLOUR TORTILLAS (6-INCH)
- 6 TABLESPOONS UNAGI (EEL) SAUCE
- 4 RED OR GOLDEN RIPE TOMATOES, SLICED INTO ROUNDS
- 1 RED ONION, SKIN REMOVED & SLIVERED
- 4 KIRBY CUCUMBERS, SLICED INTO ROUNDS
- 2 AVOCADOS, THINLY SLICED
- ARUGULA MINT SLAW (RECIPE TO FOLLOW)
- SPICY AIOLI (RECIPE TO FOLLOW)

SCORE THE SKIN of the duck breast and season with kosher salt and black pepper. Heat 1 tablespoon olive oil in a cast iron skillet over medium low heat. Once hot, place duck breast skin side down in skillet. Render the fat from the under the skin; this can take longer than expected. Once the skin is VERY crisp, turn breast over and cook until medium rare. When duck is finished, remove from skillet and let rest. Pull the skin from the duck, chop and set aside.

Use the same pan to cook the bacon and set aside.

Grill tortillas on both sides until slightly charred, but not burnt. Drizzle the bottom of each tortilla with the unagi sauce in a tic-tac-toe design. Continue pizzette assembly by layering the ingredients in this order: arugula mint slaw, 2 tomato slices, red onion slivers, 4 cucumber slices, 4 thin slices of duck breast then 4 avocado slices. Drizzle spicy aioli sauce over top and add crumbled bacon and chopped duck cracklin'. Slice pizzette into fourths and serve.

ARUGULA MINT SLAW

- 2 CUPS ARUGULA (PREFERABLY SMALL LEAVES)
- ¼ HEAD PURPLE CABBAGE, THINLY SLICED
- ¼ HEAD GREEN CABBAGE, THINLY SLICED
- ¾ CUP FRESH TORN MINT LEAVES
- 2 LARGE CARROTS, PEELED & JULIENNED
- 1 BUNCH OF CILANTRO, LEAVES ONLY, CHOPPED
- KOSHER SALT & PEPPER TO TASTE
- 1 LIME, JUICED
- ¼ CUP EXTRA VIRGIN OLIVE OIL (ADJUST AMOUNT OF OIL AS NEEDED)

PLACE ALL ingredients except lime and olive oil in a bowl and mix well. Season with salt and pepper. Drizzle lime juice and olive oil over slaw mixture and toss until incorporated (the mixture should not be very wet).

SPICY AIOLI

- 8 EGG YOLKS
- ½ CUP RICE WINE VINEGAR
- 1 BOTTLE TOGARASHI CHILE BLEND (.52-OUNCE)
- 1 TABLESPOON SESAME OIL
- 1 TABLESPOON DIJON MUSTARD
- 1 TABLESPOON SRIRACHA HOT CHILI SAUCE
- 1 LEMON, JUICED
- 4 CUPS VEGETABLE OIL
- SALT & PEPPER TO TASTE

COMBINE ALL ingredients except vegetable oil in a blender and pulse until combined. With blender running, slowly add oil and blend until emulsified. Season with salt and pepper. Keep refrigerated.

PHEASANT POT PIE

EMMA LINCOLN

SERVES 6-8

For people who hunt, I like to incorporate what they hunt into the recipes we serve them. I just try to use a little ingenuity to make something special with what people love. This recipe is based on a standard chicken pot pie recipe, but using pheasant.

PHEASANTS:

- 3 PHEASANTS
- ½ CUP SALT
- 1 ONION
- 2 CELERY STALKS
- 1 APPLE
- 1 ORANGE
- 1 CARROT

MAKE A BRINE by dissolving ½ cup of salt into 2 quarts of boiling water. Let brine cool completely and pour enough over pheasants to cover them completely (you can use a large plastic bag or container with a lid for this). Refrigerate the pheasants overnight. Drain brine, rinse pheasants and place them in pot. Cover with fresh water. Cut onions, celery, apple, orange and carrot into chunks and add to the pot. Cover and boil pheasants until done, approximately 1 hour. Remove the pheasants and allow them to cool. Cube the breast meat and set aside until time to assemble pot pie.

VEGETABLES:

- 2 MEDIUM CARROTS
- 1 MEDIUM POTATO
- 1 MEDIUM ONION
- ½ CUP FROZEN GREEN PEAS

PEEL AND CUBE the carrots and potato. Dice the onion. In a large pot, cover the carrots and potato with water and bring to a boil. Boil the carrots and potato until just fork tender, approximately 10 minutes. Add diced onion and peas and continue to boil for an additional 3 to 4 minutes. Drain and set aside.

CREAM SAUCE:

- ½ CUP BUTTER
- ½ CUP FLOUR
- 2½ CUPS CHICKEN BROTH
- 1½ CUPS WHIPPING CREAM
- ½ TEASPOON DRIED THYME
- SALT & PEPPER TO TASTE

MELT BUTTER in a saucepan over medium low heat and whisk in flour. Stir constantly for a minute and then whisk in cream and broth. Stir constantly until sauce thickens, approximately 3 minutes. Add thyme and season with salt and pepper. Set aside.

PIE CRUST:

- 2½ CUPS ALL-PURPOSE FLOUR, PLUS EXTRA FOR ROLLING
- 1 TEASPOON SALT
- 1 CUP SHORTENING, VERY COLD & CUT INTO CUBES
- 1 CUP ICE WATER
- 1 EGG YOLK MIXED WITH 1 TABLESPOON OF WATER (EGG WASH)

COMBINE FLOUR, salt and shortening in a large bowl or base of a food processor. Use your hands to cut the shortening into the flour (or pulse about 10 times in the processor) until you reach the consistency of small peas. Sprinkle the mixture with 6 tablespoons of strained ice water and pulse or mix until a smooth dough forms. If dough is too dry, you can add more water by the ½ tablespoon until dough comes together in a ball. Divide dough in half, wrap in plastic wrap and chill for 30 minutes. *(continued)*

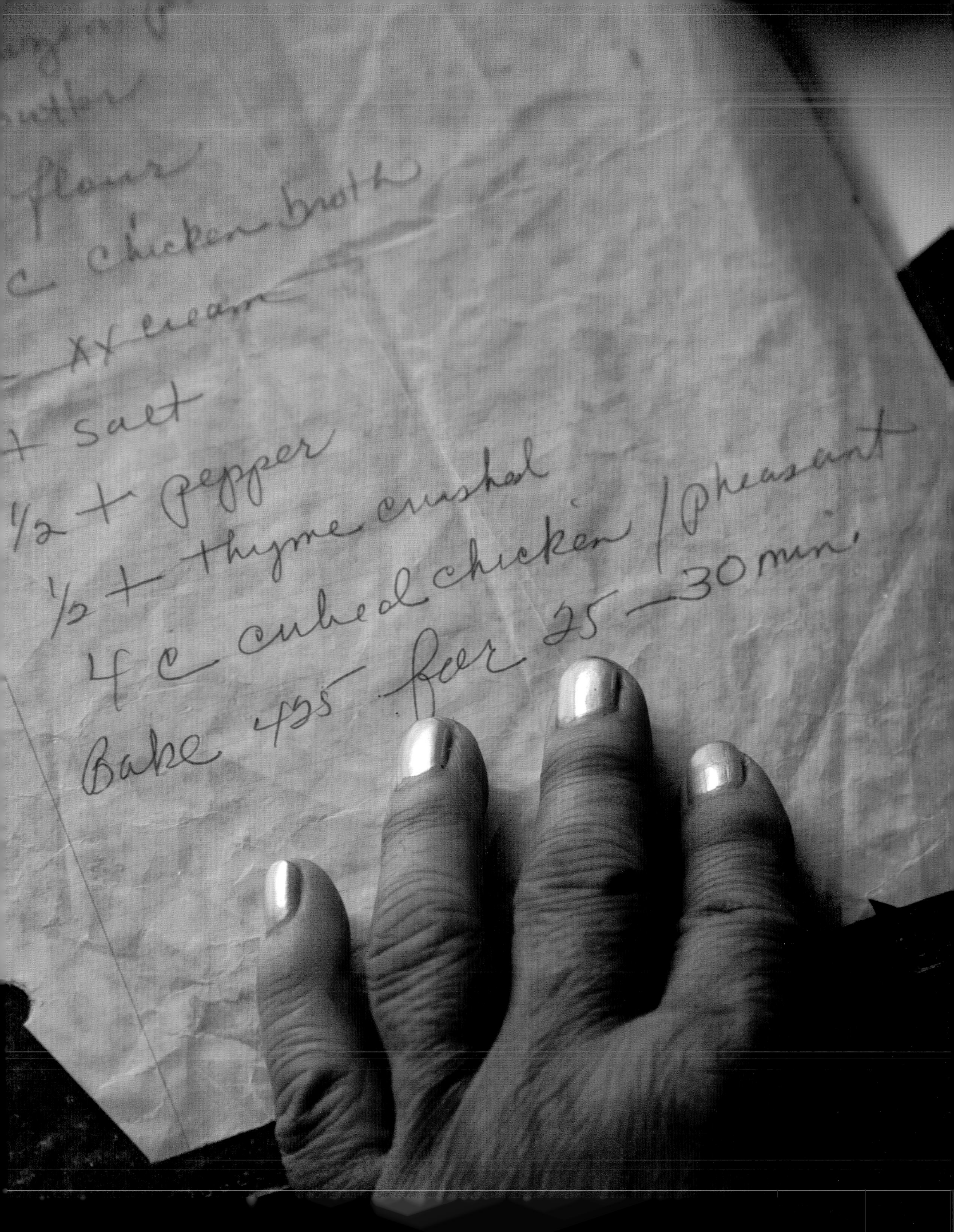

flour

c chicken broth

XX cream

+ salt

½ t pepper

½ t thyme crushed

4 c cubed chicken / Pheasant

Bake 425 - for 25 - 30 min.

ASSEMBLY:

PREHEAT OVEN to 425 degrees. Roll out each crust on a lightly floured surface to an 11 inch round. Line a 10 inch round baking dish with one of the prepared crusts. Combine cubed pheasant and vegetables in a bowl and gently mix in cream sauce. Spoon mixture into the prepared pan and cover with the second crust. Crimp edges of crusts together and brush the whole top crust with egg wash. Cut a couple of vents in the dough to release steam and bake the pie for 25 to 30 minutes or until browned. Serve hot.

NOTES:

Use your favorite store-bought pie dough or make your own. This recipe makes enough for two crusts.

This dough can be made a couple of days in advance and stored in the refrigerator. Let the dough come to room temperature (30 minutes to 1 hour) before rolling.

"Her warm smile, strong hands, nurturing ways and attention to detail in the kitchen were all I needed to realize I was meeting a gem."

HUSH PUPPIES

EMMA LINCOLN

MAKES 3-4 DOZEN

This started out as my mother's recipe, but I've added to it and evolved it over the years, so now it is really my own. One of my greatest talents as a cook and business owner is putting the right task with the right person. If Mary Frances Ingram is around Quail Hollow, the frying is her assignment. She likes to do it, she's got the patience and she is so good at frying.

NOTES:

Use a small ice cream scoop for uniform, round hush puppies.

- 2 CUPS PLAIN CORNMEAL
- 2 TABLESPOONS ALL-PURPOSE FLOUR
- 1 TEASPOON BAKING SODA
- 1 TEASPOON BAKING POWDER
- 1 TEASPOON SALT
- 2 TABLESPOONS SUGAR
- ⅓ CUP ONION, CHOPPED
- 1 EGG, BEATEN
- 1 CUP BUTTERMILK
- 3 TABLESPOONS JALAPEÑO PEPPERS, CHOPPED
- 4 TABLESPOONS MEXICORN® (CANNED CORN WITH PEPPERS, ONIONS AND SPICES)
- OIL FOR FRYING

MIX TOGETHER all dry ingredients. Stir in onion. Mix together the beaten egg and buttermilk. Add wet mixture to dry ingredients. Stir in chopped peppers and Mexicorn®. Heat 2 or 3 inches of oil in a cast iron skillet or Dutch oven until it reaches 375 degrees. Drop small spoonfuls of the batter into the hot oil.

Cook the hush puppies in batches until they are golden brown and float to the top; do not crowd the pan.

Our Mother's Table is Emma Lincoln's tribute to her mother, Beneva Mayweather, one of the finest cooks to grace many a kitchen in Memphis and beyond. Emma, and her mother before her, has been catering for the Dunavants for 30 years.

PEPPERMINT ICE CREAM

BENEVA MAYWEATHER

MAKES APPROXIMATELY 2 QUARTS

Beneva Mayweather, one of the first female chefs in the South, was ahead of her time. She started out as a cook, then sous chef and eventually executive chef at a private club in Memphis. Her nickname was "The Magician," as she had a knack for being in two places at the same time. Being hired by the club's patrons to cook on the side grew into a full-time catering business, Mayweather Catering, which Beneva started in 1973. She would cater private parties and still be able to return to the club's kitchen in time to knock out the homemade desserts. In 2007, after Beneva's death, Emma and her friend Denise Sims compiled and published *Our Mother's Table*, a collection of Beneva's recipes and a tribute to a woman so proud of her craft.

- 3 CUPS CREAM
- 2 CUPS HALF AND HALF
- 3 CUPS SOFT PEPPERMINT STICKS, CRUSHED
- 2 TEASPOONS VANILLA EXTRACT

IN A LARGE BOWL, combine cream, half and half and crushed peppermint. Mix well. Cover and refrigerate mixture until candy dissolves completely. Add vanilla and pour mixture into a hand cranked or electric ice cream machine. Freeze according to the manufacturer's directions.

NOTES:

Soft peppermint sticks (like King Leo®) work best in this recipe. If unavailable, you can substitute hard peppermint candies.

From Our Mother's Table.

CHOCOLATE SAUCE

BENEVA MAYWEATHER

YIELDS APPROXIMATELY 1 CUP

NOTES:

Some recipe testers prefer to whisk in the sugar after the chocolate, cream and water are melted; ensuring the sugar is fully dissolved.

From Our Mother's Table.

- 4 OUNCES UNSWEETENED CHOCOLATE, CHOPPED
- 1 ⅔ CUP SUGAR
- ½ CUP CREAM
- ¼ CUP HOT WATER
- 2 TEASPOONS VANILLA EXTRACT
- PINCH OF SALT

COMBINE CHOCOLATE, sugar, cream and water in a saucepan over medium low heat. Stir constantly until mixture is smooth and thickened (approximately 8 minutes). Remove from heat, cool and stir in vanilla.

SMOKED DUCK QUESADILLAS EMMA LINCOLN

SERVES 8

My sister came up with this recipe years ago. She went to the California Culinary Academy, where the instructors encourage experimentation. At the Dunavants' Christmas parties, we always liked to use wild turkey because that's what Mr. Dunavant hunts and what he likes. One Christmas my sister was home and suggested smoking the duck and making quesadillas. Instead of just cooking the duck, we smoked it, which gave it more flavor.

- 1½ CUPS SMOKED DUCK BREAST MEAT
- 8 FLOUR TORTILLAS (8 INCH)
- 2 CUPS PEPPER JACK CHEESE, GRATED

PREHEAT OVEN to 400 degrees. Place 4 tortillas on a greased cookie sheet and divide duck meat evenly over tortillas. Sprinkle with pepper jack cheese and top with the additional tortillas. Bake for 10 to 15 minutes until cheese melts. Cut quesadillas into quarters and serve.

NOTES:

For better flavor, Emma prefers to use duck seasoned well with salt and pepper and slow cooked in a smoker for 1 to 1½ hours. Once the ducks have cooled, remove breast meat and slice very thinly. Any type of cooked duck will work in this recipe, though, and it is a great way to use leftover duck meat.

Wesley Ross, keeper of the lodge, lives on the property, cleans the game and fries the catfish and chicken. "Our family memories were made on screened-in porches."

VENISON FINGERS WITH CUMBERLAND SAUCE

KAREN CARRIER

SERVES 4-6 AS AN APPETIZER

This recipe is in memory of my dear friend Pete Hood from Shreveport, Louisiana. We were students together at the Memphis Academy of Arts and both moved to New York City after school. During my early years in Manhattan, he would throw fantastic dinner parties in his tiny, two-room apartment. On occasion Pete would receive packages from his folks down South filled with wild venison meat. I grew up in a kosher, orthodox Jewish home with an English mom and a Polish-descended dad. Needless to say, I had never eaten wild or domestic game at my young age of 18. Pete was an incredible, truly inspirational cook. Every year Pete would make this special dinner. To this day I can remember him standing over the stove with his dark, blue-black hair, giving me that great smile and telling us about this traditional family recipe and his family's hunting escapades.

I got a call the other day from a mutual friend of ours saying that my dear friend Pete had passed away. Many memories came flooding back, and of all the decadent stories we shared in the 1970s and 1980s, this sweet memory of Pete preparing venison fingers stands out in my mind. Thanks, Pete, for many great dinners, laugh-out-loud stories and sharing your wonderful food traditions along the way.

VENISON FINGERS

- 1 POUND WILD VENISON TENDERLOIN
- ¼ TEASPOON CINNAMON
- 2 CUPS BUTTERMILK
- 2 CUPS ALL-PURPOSE FLOUR
- ½ TEASPOON KOSHER SALT
- ½ TEASPOON BLACK PEPPER
- ½ TEASPOON SEASONED SALT
- 1 PINCH OF CAYENNE PEPPER
- ½ TO 1 CUP OF PEANUT OIL FOR FRYING

RINSE AND PAT DRY venison and cut into small, bite sized chunks. Mix together cinnamon and buttermilk. Add the meat and marinate for 4 hours in the fridge.

Mix flour, salt, pepper, seasoned salt and cayenne pepper.

Add peanut oil to a skillet or Dutch oven over medium high heat to approximately 350 degrees. Remove venison pieces from buttermilk marinade and thoroughly coat them in the seasoned flour mixture. Gently drop venison into the skillet and fry for 5 minutes, turning occasionally until nuggets are golden brown.

CUMBERLAND DIPPING SAUCE

- 1 TEASPOON DRY MUSTARD
- 1 TABLESPOON BROWN SUGAR
- ¼ TEASPOON POWDERED GINGER
- 1 PINCH OF CAYENNE PEPPER
- ¼ TEASPOON KOSHER SALT
- ¼ TEASPOON GROUND CLOVES
- 1½ CUPS PORT
- ½ CUP RAISINS
- ½ CUP SLIVERED ALMONDS
- 2 TEASPOONS CORNSTARCH
- 2 TABLESPOONS COLD WATER
- ¼ CUP RED CURRANT JELLY
- 1 TABLESPOON ORANGE OR LEMON ZEST
- ¼ CUP ORANGE JUICE
- 2 TABLESPOONS LEMON JUICE

COMBINE FIRST NINE ingredients (mustard through almonds) in a small pot; cover and simmer for 8 minutes. In a small bowl, dissolve cornstarch into water and stir this into sauce. Simmer for 2 minutes. Stir in remaining ingredients to finish the sauce.

"Emma asked me to beat the duck for country fried duck, and I was ready."

"Now this is the size of a wild turkey!" says Emma Lincoln.

"The heart of the matter is always in the kitchen." Karen Carrier and Tommie Dunavant

"This was an extended family…how lucky I was to be a part of its history."
(l to r) Tommie Dunavant, Billy Dunavant and Emma Lincoln

MARTHA FOOSE

WITH CHRIS ROBINSON
AT WARD LAKE

A brace of ducks on the porch reflects the sunset and spirit of Ward Lake.

ON A DIM JANUARY twilight's last gleaming, I pulled down the spine of the levee running through the boggy bottoms of the Mississippi Delta. Arriving at Ward Lake Hunting Club, a 6,500-acre preserve near Clarksdale, I pulled up to a modest camp house overlooking a cypress hole. Piled next to the front stairs were six walking sticks carved with intricate talismans. A sign, I supposed, that I had come to the right place. In moments the door swung open, and I entered the warren of the Swamp Witches.

WITH A NAME LIKE SWAMP WITCHES, cackling, evil laughter might be what one would expect to ring through the mist, but what echoed through this bayou evening were howls of laughter and high-pitched giggles. Allison Crews is the Queen Witch, and along a roundabout path assembled a circle of girlfriends who, for more than a decade, have congregated several times a year at her family's place. The one fellow allowed to come along, with the understanding that he'd be spending a good deal of time in the kitchen, was cook Chris Robinson, brought into the fold by way of friendship with a couple of the Swamp Witches' husbands. A much coveted invitation got me a place at the table and a memorable meal served with unforgettable stories.

As Susan Williams unpacked the hand-thrown earthenware to set the table, she lamented that this would be their last dinner at this cabin. The crew is moving to another house down the road. The décor of this place, a cross between *Sports Afield* and Pottery Barn, had a traditional duck camp feel with decidedly feminine touches. Their dress was much the same. Lind Bussey and Leigh Bailey sported traditional Swamp Witch-wear (layers of mismatched camouflage and earth tones) topped with fur caps – every conceivable design and variety of pelt is welcomed. Witch Kate Morrison came with her new pup, Rosie, while Lila Sessums provided wry commentary with her lab, Tuff, by her side.

As the ladies caught up with each other, Chris whipped up a game dinner par excellence – remaining unflappable as a cyclone of dogs and women swarmed in and out of his kitchen, all sniffing around for a bite. At this hunting camp, a cook has to improvise a good deal. Chris may toss a salad in a skillet for lack of a bowl or come up with a creative substitute for an ingredient left back in town. He seems to roll with the punches. He makes things work because he wants to take care of his ladies. He makes a hearty feast that has become almost ritual – creating the meal that serves as the centerpiece for their lively storytelling and giving them sustenance for the early morning hunt ahead.

WARD LAKE HUNTING CLUB

THE SWAMP WITCHES are a group of women who gather two or three times each season at the Ward Lake Hunting Club in Sherard, Mississippi. Under the leadership of James M. Crews, Jr., father-in-law of Queen Witch Allison Crews, members of the club acquired the 6,500-acre conservation parcel in a series of purchases from the mid-1980s to 2001. Besides Allison Crews, the Swamp Witches include Mississippians Leigh Bailey, Lind Bussey, Lila Sessums and Susan Williams, as well as Kate Morrison from Memphis.

MARTHA FOOSE

GIFTED CHEF and storyteller Martha Foose's *Screen Doors and Sweet Tea* was the 2009 James Beard Award winner for best American cookbook. Martha, also author of *A Southerly Course: Recipes and Stories from Close to Home* and former executive chef of the Viking Cooking School in Greenwood, Mississippi, was born and raised in the Mississippi Delta and now lives in Tchula. She attended the renowned pastry school École Lenôtre in France. Upon returning to Mississippi, Martha opened Bottletree Bakery – a Southern institution in Oxford – and later, with her husband, Mockingbird Bakery in Greenwood.

CHRIS ROBINSON

NOW IN RESIDENTIAL real estate, Chris Robinson has spent most of his lifetime in the food business. A native Memphian, he grew up working at his family's catering company and restaurant, Monte's, before attending the University of Memphis and La Maison Meridian, a local culinary school. He has experience as a corporate chef for Kroger, chef at a private club in Memphis and director of food service for a hospital. Having grown up hunting and fishing, he has a passion for both and enjoys private cooking engagements at hunting clubs.

A game dinner from Chris Robinson, who makes things work despite the swarm of ladies in and out of his kitchen

"A cross between *Sports Afield* and Pottery Barn...with decidedly feminine touches"

While Chris put the finishing touches on dinner, the hunters headed to the mud room, organized the gear and turned waders down in preparation for morning. I was told that a few Witches sleep in their long underwear and camo so they just have to slip into waiting waders in the predawn. All agreed it was best to take care of business before it got too late in the evening or anyone got too deep in her cups. It was around this time Lila chimed in that she better get old Tuff ready, too, "before I'm too drunk to dress my dog for dinner." While Lila outfitted Tuff in a ridiculous costume that resembled Elton John from the 1970s, Chris hollered from the kitchen, "I once had a dog who would only eat Red Starlin' Darlin' Hot Dogs!" This didn't seem like anything new to them. They certainly weren't showing off for my benefit. It was just the raucous, rollicking nature of the camp.

After readying everything for the morning, dinner was soon served. Before the meal, Allison said grace. "Thank you for your glorious outdoors," she prayed, and whispered "Amens" swirled around the table. At dinner I tried to track how this sisterhood was formed. All agreed that Allison, soon joined by Kate, were the first. Then twists and turns and happenstance brought the rest into the fold. All were initially united by love for horses and the sporting nature of fox hunting. But like directions to a good duck hole, it was not as simple a road as it sounds. Their recollections of the early days of friendship were punctuated by laughter with deadpan delivery of lines like, "I bought her horse the day after she made me ride in a parade. She did ask me if I wanted to ride *before* or *after* the fire truck…" and good-natured ribbing: "I saw posted on the bulletin board at the tack shop, 'Horse for Sale. Call Lila Lavigne.' Sounded like a stripper name Li-la Le-veeene…" Their escapades are not confined to duck season and fox hunting alone. These gals are game for adventure in any season. The plight of the elusive club-footed turkey had a couple of them rearranging work schedules after a turkey call was answered on a weekday pre-work hunt (business attire worn under the camo). There was the wild boar hunt that saw a black hog as big as a pony taken down with a steel-sighted World War I Mauser. None of this came off as bragging, just as jubilant reminiscences.

By the time Chris presented a store-bought princess cake for dessert he deemed "rich enough to have a credit rating," we were all blushed with wine, and the stories had drifted from silly to sentimental. It hasn't been all laughs and hijinks for these friends. They have seen one another through some tough spots. Life-threatening injuries and illnesses have cemented their bonds. I learned around that dinner table that the Swamp Witches are six accomplished women dedicated to hunting and to each other.

They are a group bound by their appreciation of sport, affection for each other and love of a good time and a good laugh. The Swamp Witches like to pull one over on the uninitiated, introducing Allison's dog, Crockett, to each guest by name at the beginning of the hunt and then having him deliver personalized breakfast by swimming a biscuit wrapped in a zip-top bag out to each hunter in the blind (achieved with sly hand signals). Biscuit breakfast is a ritual for the Witches. Instead of a cauldron, Queen Witch Allison presides over a beat-up propane camp stove with a good coating of swamp sludge set up in her aged canoe. Strict adherence to this sacrament must be followed. Pillsbury® Grands! biscuits cooked three-quarters of the way through are the only variety allowed. As I was told, it is the only kind that brown just right on the old stove and hold up to the various modes of delivery, which include the aforementioned dog or ferried on canoe paddles. Chris sets the ladies up the night before with leftovers to swaddle in the biscuits – be they lamb chops, pork chops or venison sausages with a bottle of honey mustard. One morning he even had lobster and crab cakes for the ladies to insert into their warmed-over biscuits. This is not a fried bologna sandwich and trolling motor gang. These purists eschew newfangled duck boats, favoring canoes to haul their decoys and gear. Eyeing the sky from beneath the brim of their chic tartan-banded hats, these experienced hunters can call a mallard by its wing action. They aren't pantywaists. That being said, they may refer to a banded duck as wearing jewelry. This chapter and these recipes are dedicated to the one-of-a-kind Swamp Witches: Allison, Susan, Kate, Lind, Leigh and Lila; I have fallen under their spell. ❀

"A much coveted invitation got me a place at the table and…unforgettable stories." (clockwise from l) Tuff Sessums, Lila Sessums, Susan Williams, Martha Foose, Allison Crews, guest Cortney Viglietti, guest Susan Schadt, Kate Morrison, Leigh Bailey and Lind Bussey

The lone fellow, Ward Lake Warlock Chris Robinson, and Martha Foose whip up dinner in the warren's kitchen.

ASIAN-STYLE ELK MEATBALLS CHRIS ROBINSON

MAKES APPROXIMATELY 50 APPETIZER MEATBALLS

As a kid working at my family's restaurant, Monte's, I made countless meatballs with sweet tomato sauce. Years later, a hunting friend had some ground elk, and I thought doing a meatball out of it would be a good appetizer. I liked the idea of mixing savory meatballs with a sweet sauce, as we had done at Monte's, but introduced an Asian flavor to the dish with the hoisin sauce.

- 2 EGGS, LIGHTLY BEATEN
- 1 CUP SALTINE CRACKERS, CRUSHED
- ½ CUP COOKED RICE
- 1 TABLESPOON GARLIC, CHOPPED
- 2 POUNDS GROUND ELK MEAT
- OLIVE OIL FOR SEARING
- 1 TABLESPOON SALT
- 1½ TEASPOONS BLACK PEPPER
- 1 18-OUNCE JAR HOISIN SAUCE

NOTES:

Almost any game meat and be substituted for elk in this recipe.

PREHEAT OVEN to 350 degrees. Combine eggs, cracker crumbs, rice and garlic in a large bowl and gently fold in meat. Season with salt and pepper. Measure approximately 1 tablespoon sized portions of the mixture and roll into balls. Heat a large skillet over medium heat and cover with a thin layer of olive oil. Sear the meatballs on all sides in batches; do not crowd the pan. Add more oil as needed. Place meatballs on a baking sheet and cook until done all the way through, approximately 15 minutes. Heat hoisin sauce in a small saucepan and pour over meatballs before serving.

BRAISED VENISON SHANKS CHRIS ROBINSON

SERVES 10

Growing up, I always hated game because it typically was so overcooked. When I went to culinary school, I was trained in the classics – country French and northern Italian – and learned techniques and cooking methods, like braising, that really brought out the flavor in food. I worked at a private club and adapted one of its signature dishes, lamb shanks, into braised venison shanks by using a slow-cook method to maximize the flavor of the game meat.

- 10 VENISON SHANKS
- 5 TABLESPOONS OLIVE OIL
- SALT & PEPPER TO TASTE
- 3 QUARTS BEEF DEMI-GLACE
- 10 OUNCES DRY RED WINE
- 3-4 TABLESPOONS GARLIC, CHOPPED
- 15 MEDIUM SIZED SHALLOTS, PEELED

NOTES:

Demi-glace can be purchased at gourmet shops and most upscale grocery stores. If demi-glace is not available, use good quality beef stock. This sauce makes a great base for many additions. Try mushrooms, herbs or diced tomatoes.

You can substitute veal shanks for venison.

PREHEAT OVEN to 400 degrees. Heat a Dutch oven over high heat until very hot, approximately 3 minutes. Rub shanks with olive oil, salt and pepper and sear them in the Dutch oven on all sides. Brown the meat only; do not fully cook. Remove shanks from pan.

Bring demi-glace, wine, garlic and peeled shallots to a simmer in Dutch oven. Add shanks back and cover. Cook in the oven until fork tender, approximately 1½ to 2 hours.

KALE AND BLACK-EYED PEAS   MARTHA FOOSE

SERVES 6-8

If you are ever lucky enough to get to hang out in a kitchen with Susan telling hunting tales, put these peas on to simmer and sit back for some exciting, animated stories.

From *A Southerly Course: Recipes and Stories from Close to Home,* Clarkson Potter 2011.

- 1 QUART FRESH SHELLED OR FROZEN & THAWED BLACK-EYED PEAS
- 1 SMOKED HAM HOCK
- 3 CUPS WATER
- 1 SMALL ONION, CHOPPED
- 1 HEAD KALE, STEMS & VEINS REMOVED & LEAVES CHOPPED
- 2-4 TABLESPOONS BUTTER
- SALT & PEPPER TO TASTE

RINSE AND PICK through peas. In a large saucepan over medium high heat, boil ham hock in water for 15 minutes. Spoon off any scum that rises. Add onion, peas and kale. Reduce heat to a simmer and cook 20 minutes. Add butter and season with salt and pepper. Cook for an additional 15 to 20 minutes or until peas are quite tender. Adjust seasoning. Serve with store-bought vinegar pepper sauce or Vera Williams' Sport Sauce on page 167.

PINE NUT PESTO   MARTHA FOOSE

MAKES APPROXIMATELY 1 CUP

Leigh's hospitable nature inspired this dish. Like the pesto, she is quick and has great taste. This pesto is great on pasta or spooned over cream cheese or goat cheese for a quick appetizer.

NOTES:

This pesto freezes beautifully. Cover the top of the pesto with a thin layer of olive oil to prevent browning.

From *A Southerly Course: Recipes and Stories from Close to Home,* Clarkson Potter 2011.

- 1 CUP FRESH BASIL LEAVES, WASHED & DRIED
- ½ CUP SPINACH LEAVES, WASHED & DRIED
- 6 PARSLEY SPRIGS, LEAVES ONLY
- 3 MARJORAM SPRIGS, LEAVES ONLY
- 1/2 CUP PINE NUTS
- 2-3 GARLIC CLOVES, PRESSED (USE GARLIC PRESS)
- ⅓ CUP PARMESAN CHEESE, GRATED
- ¼-⅓ CUP OLIVE OIL
- 2 TABLESPOONS BUTTER, SOFTENED
- ¼ TEASPOON SALT

COMBINE ALL INGREDIENTS in a blender or food processor and pulse until smooth.

"Every conceivable design and variety of pelt is welcomed." (bottom row, l to r) Lila Sessums, Allison Crews, Susan Williams, Martha Foose; (top row, l to r) Leigh Bailey, Chris Robinson, Lind Bussey, and Kate Morrison

Martha Foose's visit with the Swamp Witches marked their last dinner in the former clubhouse. Allison and Jim Crews have a new cabin on the lake (at left) where all Swamp Witch dinners will take place.

Susan Williams' interchangable "in or out" hat

The devil's in the details: Kate Morrison

"In the course of telling a tale about a previous season's hunt, Lila slapped the table for emphasis (retriever-speak for 'Kennel Up!'). With that, Tuff immediately bound upon the table, sending wine glasses flying. He didn't know she was telling a story; he just knew Lila had 'said' the magic words. We all about fell out of our chairs with laughter as Tuff stood baffled on the dinner table, standing in a puddle of Burgundy with a slightly embarrassed look on his face."

BURGUNDY DUCK

MARTHA FOOSE

SERVES 10

I'll never forget the look on Lila's face when Tuff jumped on the dinner table. Red wine and duck are always good together!

NOTES:

You may wonder why you brown the ducks on all sides if the skin is getting discarded. Because it adds tons of flavor and makes the dish taste good!

From *A Southerly Course: Recipes and Stories from Close to Home,* Clarkson Potter 2011.

- 2 WHOLE (1-POUND) WILD DUCKS OR 8 (4-OUNCE) DUCK BREASTS
- 4 TABLESPOONS UNSALTED BUTTER
- ¼ CUP UNBLEACHED ALL-PURPOSE FLOUR
- 2 CUPS CHICKEN BROTH
- 1 CUP RED WINE, PREFERABLY BURGUNDY
- 2 SHALLOTS, CHOPPED
- 2 BAY LEAVES
- 2 CUPS WHITE MUSHROOMS, CHOPPED
- SALT & PEPPER TO TASTE
- MELBA TOAST FOR SERVING

PUT DUCKS in a large pot, cover them with water and season water with salt. Simmer over medium heat for 30 minutes. Drain, remove ducks and pat them dry.

Return pot to the stove, add butter and melt over medium high heat. Add ducks and cook, turning occasionally, for 15 minutes and brown on all sides. Transfer to a plate and set aside to cool. Remove the skin, discard the bones and shred the meat.

Add flour to pot and stir constantly for 2 minutes over medium heat. Whisk in broth, wine, shallots and bay leaves. Add mushrooms and season with salt and pepper. Stir for 5 minutes or until the mixture is slightly thick and beginning to bubble. Return ducks to pot and cover. Reduce heat to low and cook for 1 hour.

Serve warm heaped on Melba toast.

SOUR CREAM BISCUITS

MARTHA FOOSE

MAKES APPROXIMATELY 1 DOZEN

This recipe can come in handy in case somebody forgets to pack the biscuits. These are also good for snacking, snuggled up with one of Allison's novels in front of the fire.

From *A Southerly Course: Recipes and Stories from Close to Home,* Clarkson Potter 2011.

- 2 CUPS UNBLEACHED ALL-PURPOSE FLOUR, PLUS EXTRA FOR SHAPING BISCUITS
- 1 TABLESPOON BAKING POWDER
- ½ TEASPOON BAKING SODA
- ½ TEASPOON SALT
- 1 CUP SOUR CREAM

PREHEAT THE OVEN to 450 degrees. Mix together flour, baking powder, baking soda and salt. Add sour cream and mix until a soft dough forms. With well-floured hands, gently shape the dough into 2 inch rounds. Place on a cookie sheet and bake for 9 to 12 minutes or until barely browned.

TOMATO RELISH FRITTERS

MARTHA FOOSE

MAKES APPROXIMATELY 14 FRITTERS

These fritters are wonderful served alongside any game dish. The tomato relish is easy to keep on hand in the pantry. I bet Kate's new pup will eat up these fancy hush puppies!

NOTES:

Tomato relish can be found at most farmer's markets or gourmet food stores. If unavailable, try substituting equal parts of freshly diced tomato and red pepper relish.

From *A Southerly Course: Recipes and Stories from Close to Home,* Clarkson Potter 2011.

- 2 CUPS SELF-RISING CORNMEAL
- ½ CUP SELF-RISING FLOUR
- ½ TEASPOON SALT
- ¼ TEASPOON SUGAR
- ½ CUP ONION, GRATED
- 1 CUP STORE-BOUGHT TOMATO RELISH, DRAINED
- 1 CUP BUTTERMILK
- 1 EGG
- OIL FOR FRYING

IN A MIXING BOWL, whisk together cornmeal, flour, salt and sugar to remove any lumps. In a separate bowl, combine onion, relish, buttermilk and egg. Mix wet ingredients into the dry and stir well to combine. Let batter rest for 15 minutes.

Meanwhile, heat fryer or 3 inches of frying oil in a deep pot to 375 degrees.

Do not stir batter. Dip two tablespoons into hot oil. Spoon one full of batter and use the other spoon to slide mixture off into the hot oil. Continue to form and drop more fritters, re-dipping the spoons if they become too thick with batter. Cook fritters until crisped and browned, turning as needed, for 2 to 3 minutes. Do not crowd the pan. Drain fritters on a wire rack set over newspaper or a paper sack, and serve hot.

Wild boar hunt stories of "a black hog as big as a pony":
Lila Sessums and Susan Williams

Ka-boom! A steel-sighted World War I Mauser, jubilant reminiscences:
(l to r) Martha Foose, Chris Robinson and Lila Sessums

Tuff and Lila Sessums

BLUEBERRY COBBLER

MARTHA FOOSE

SERVES 4-6

Maybe it's her blue eyes or maybe it's her sweet disposition. This cobbler seems just right for Lind.

- ½ CUP BUTTER
- 1 PINT FRESH OR FROZEN BLUEBERRIES
- 1 TEASPOON FRESHLY SQUEEZED LEMON JUICE
- ¼ CUP WATER
- 2 CUPS SUGAR, DIVIDED
- 1 CUP SELF-RISING FLOUR
- ½ CUP MILK
- ½ TEASPOON VANILLA EXTRACT

PREHEAT OVEN to 375 degrees.

Melt butter (in oven) in an 8x8 or other deep dish baking pan.

In a saucepan, combine blueberries, lemon juice, water and 1 cup sugar. Bring to a boil and remove from heat.

For the batter, combine 1 cup sugar and remaining ingredients, mixing until smooth. Pour over the melted butter in the baking pan. Top evenly with the blueberry mixture.

Bake until top is golden brown and crusty, about 25 to 30 minutes.

NOTES:

If self-rising flour is not on hand, combine 1 teaspoon baking powder and ½ teaspoon salt with 1 cup all-purpose flour.

From A Southerly Course: Recipes and Stories from Close to Home, Clarkson Potter 2011.

"This chapter and these recipes are dedicated to the one-of-a-kind Swamp Witches; I have fallen under their spell."

Howls of laughter abound: wry humor from Lila Sessums and Martha Foose

Guest Susan Schadt, Lind Bussey, Allison Crews and Leigh Bailey (seated)

The elusive club-footed turkey story:
(l to r) Susan Williams, Lila Sessums and Martha Foose

"A group bound by their appreciation of sport, affection for each other and love of a good time and a good laugh": Allison Crews and Leigh Bailey

The all-female group is a rarity in the duck hunting world. The Swamp Witches have received significant national press attention and host a Web site, swampwitches.com. An article about their "duck hunting sorority" appeared in a 2009 issue of *The New York Times*, and the Swamp Witches have been featured in the magazines *Women in the Outdoors*, *Outdoor Life* and *Shooting Sportsman* and on the Web sites of ESPN and *Field & Stream*.

"Accomplished women dedicated to hunting and to each other": (top row, l to r) Lila Sessums, Kate Morrison, Susan Williams, guest Caroline Johnson, Leigh Bailey: (bottom row, l to r) Lind Bussey and Allison Crews

RESOURCE GUIDE

THE BAYOU CLUB

August
301 Tchoupitoulas Street
New Orleans,
Louisiana 70130
(504) 299-9777
restaurantaugust.com

Besh Steak
Harrah's New Orleans
228 Poydras Street
New Orleans,
Louisiana 70130
(504) 533-6111
harrahsneworleans.com

Lüke
333 St. Charles Avenue
New Orleans,
Louisiana 70130
(504) 378-2840
lukeneworleans.com

La Provence
25020 Highway 190
Lacombe, Louisiana 70445
(985) 626-7662
laprovencerestaurant.com

The American Sector
The National WWII Museum
945 Magazine Street
New Orleans,
Louisiana 70130
(504) 528-1940
nationalww2museum.org/
american-sector/

Domenica
123 Baronne Street
New Orleans,
Louisiana 70112
(504) 648-6020
domenicarestaurant.com

My New Orleans
http://shop.chefjohnbesh.com/

Shucks! The Louisiana
Seafood House
701 W. Port Street
Abbeville, Louisiana 70510
(337) 898-3311
shucksrestaurant.com

Tabasco® Pepper
Sauce Factory
Avery Island,
Louisiana 70513
(337) 365-8173
tabasco.com

BLACKFISH
HUNTING CLUB

Elfo's Restaurant
2285 S. Germantown Road
Germantown,
Tennessee 38138
(901) 753-4017
elfosrestaurant.com

CIRCLE T

Ashley's
Capital Bar and Grill
The Capital Hotel
111 West Markham Street
Little Rock, Arkansas 72201
(501) 370-7011
capitalhotel.com/
Ashleyswebsite/

FIGHTING BAYOU
HUNTING CLUB

Walker's Drive-In
3016 N. State Street
Jackson, Mississippi 39216
(601) 982-2633
walkersdrivein.com

Local 463 Urban Kitchen
121A Colony Crossing
Madison, Mississippi 39110
(601) 707-7684
local463.com

GRANDE VIEW
LODGE

Herbsaint
701 St. Charles Avenue
New Orleans,
Louisiana 70130
(504) 524-4114
herbsaint.com

Cochon
930 Tchoupitoulas Street
New Orleans,
Louisiana 70130
(504) 588-2123
cochonrestaurant.com

Cochon Butcher
930 Tchoupitoulas Street
New Orleans,
Louisiana 70130
(504) 588-PORK
cochonbutcher.com

Calcasieu
930 Tchoupitoulas Street
New Orleans,
Louisiana 70130
(504) 588-2188
calcasieurooms.com

Real Cajun
linkrestaurantgroup.com

Chef John Folse & Company
2517 South Philippe Avenue
Gonzalez, Louisiana 70737
(225) 644-6000
jfolse.com

MALLARD REST

City Grocery
152 Courthouse Square
Oxford, Mississippi 38655
(662) 232-8080
citygroceryonline.com

Bouré
309 North Lamar Boulevard
Oxford, Mississippi 38655
(662) 234-1968
citygroceryonline.com/
restaurant.php?boure

Big Bad Breakfast
719 North Lamar Boulevard
Oxford, Mississippi 38655
(662) 236-2666
citygroceryonline.com/
restaurant.php?bbb

Snackbar
721 North Lamar Boulevard
Oxford, Mississippi 38655
(662) 236-6363
citygroceryonline.com/
restaurant.php?snackbar

Webb Diner
107 E. Main Street
Webb, Mississippi 38966
(662) 375-8463

MENASHA HUNTING
& FISHING CLUB

Restaurant Iris
2146 Monroe Avenue
Memphis, Tennessee 38104
(901) 590-2828
restaurantiris.com

QUAIL HOLLOW

Another Roadside
Attraction Catering
679 Adams Avenue
Memphis, Tennessee 38105
(901) 525-2624

The Beauty Shop
Restaurant and Lounge
966 South Cooper Street
Memphis, Tennessee 38104
(901) 272-7111
thebeautyshoprestaurant.com

Dō Sushi + Noodles
964 South Cooper Street
Memphis, Tennessee 38104
(901) 272-0830
dosushimemphis.com

Mollie Fontaine Lounge
679 Adams Avenue
Memphis, Tennessee 38105
(901) 524-1886
molliefontainelounge.com

Our Mother's Table
Emma Lincoln Catering
1259 Greenwood Street
Memphis, Tennessee 38106
(901) 947-4528
ourmotherstable.com

WARD LAKE
HUNTING CLUB

*Screen Doors and Sweet Tea
A Southerly Course: Recipes
and Stories from Close to Home*
310 Kenneth Street
Greenwood,
Mississippi 38930
marthafoose.com

PRODUCTS

Benton's Smoky Mountain
Country Hams
2603 Highway 411
Madisonville,
Tennessee 37354
(423) 442-5003
bentonshams.com

D'Artagnan, Inc.
280 Wilson Avenue
Newark, New Jersey 07105
(800) 327-8246
dartagnan.com

Grimaud Farms
1320-A South Aurora Street
Stockton, California 95206
(800) 466-9955
grimaudfarms.com

Lee Hong Co. General Store
1294 Main Street
Louise, Mississippi 39097
(662) 836-5131
hooversauce.com

Hudson Valley Foie Gras
80 Brooks Road
Ferndale, New York 12734
(845) 292-2500
hudsonvalleyfoiegras.com

Maghí Extra Virgin Olive Oil
Lisa Mallory Interior Design
3092 Poplar Avenue #12
Memphis, Tennessee 38111
(901) 452-5575
lisamallorydesign.com

War Eagle Mill
11045 War Eagle Road
Rogers, Arkansas 72756
(479) 789-5343
wareaglemill.com

ACKNOWLEDGEMENTS

Deadlines and duck blinds don't scare me, but double boilers do. Coordinating and creating a cookbook with renowned chefs, cooks and hunters is not for the meek. But through these nine months with culinary and conservation geniuses, I learned a valuable lesson – not how to make a roux, but how to evoke greatness. With their spirit of adventure, talent, perseverance, the purest ingredients and heart, a recipe is completely failsafe and surely memorable.

I present my recipe for success (mix equal parts):

VOLUNTEER COMMITTEE:
The *Conservation Through Art* steering committee: Tommie & Billy Dunavant, Elizabeth & Trow Gillespie, Snow & Henry Morgan, Susan & Chuck Smith and Anne & John Stokes

CLUB MEMBERS & LODGE OWNERS:
Allison Crews, Billy Dunavant, Skipper Jernigan, George Lotterhos, Jim McGehee, Paul McIlhenny, Chuck Smith, John Stokes and Richard Zuschlag

CHEFS, COOKS, GUIDES & CLUB MANAGERS:
(Pages 10 – 273)

PHOTOGRAPHERS:
Lisa Buser, Michael Juiliano, Murray Riss and Will Smith

ARTSMEMPHIS STAFF:
Julia McDonald and Cortney Viglietti

BOOK DESIGNERS:
DOXA: Tim Walker, Ryan Slone, Corrie Blair and Charlie Hughes

RECIPE EDITOR & TESTERS:
Mimsie Crump, Lauren Boyer and Macrae Schaffler

PUBLICISTS:
Cornbread Consulting: Carol Puckett and Thomas Williams

HOSTS:
Lee Richardson and the Capital Hotel

DRIVER:
Chuck Schadt (Mr. Daisy)

PHOTOGRAPHER LISA BUSER

Memphis-based photojournalist Lisa Waddell Buser has more than 20 years experience in commercial, advertising and newspaper photography. She worked at *The Commercial Appeal* in Memphis, where she served as staff photographer, picture editor and photographer assignments editor for 11 years. She was named Newspaper Photographer of the Year by the National Press Photographers Association and won honorable mention in the Scripps Howard Photographer of the Year contest. She was a member of *The Commercial Appeal*'s photograph editing team that received the Best Use of Photography Award and the Angus McDougall Award for Excellence in Editing in the National Pictures of the Year competition.

Lisa's work has appeared in the books *Tennessee: A Homecoming, America 24/7, Tennessee 24/7* and *Missouri 24/7*. Her clients include *USA Today*, Food Network, CNN, Random House Publishing Group, Nike Inc. and Le Bonheur Children's Hospital. She and her husband live in Memphis and have two children.

PHOTOGRAPHER WILL SMITH
(*Ward Lake chapter*)
Will Smith grew up in the woods and waters of Mississippi. While attending Mississippi State University, a dear friend put a camera in his hand. Very seldom has it left. For the past 15 years, Smith has enjoyed photographing life in the Deep South, the Caribbean and South America. Smith's work has appeared in *USA Today, The New York Times, The Los Angeles Times, The Washington Post, The Clarion-Ledger, Mississippi Magazine* and numerous publications around the country and world through his work with The Associated Press. Smith's momma is a very good cook.

INDEX

front row, l to r: Susan Schadt, Julie Spear, Peggy Jalenak, Mary Berol, Karen Carrier, Emma Lincoln, Anne Stokes, Allison Garrott;
middle row, l to r: Selden Popwell, Meg Clifton, Bridget Trenary, Barbara Biedenharn, Missy Rainer, Chey Widdop, Debbie Lewis, Leslie Dunavant, Michelle Dunavant, Deborah Dunklin Tipton, Elizabeth Gillespie, Libby Dorris, Nancy Morrow, Cortney Viglietti;
top row, l to r: Elizabeth Rouse, Sarah Haizlip, Susan Smith, Julia McDonald, Julie Hussey, Anna Wunderlich, Anne Dunavant, Barbara Williamson, Tommie Dunavant, Brenda Crain, Bonnie Smith and Diane Rudner

WOMEN IN CAMO

Connie Abston	Leslie Dunavant	Julie Hussey	Jean Norfleet	Julie Spear
Connie Adams	Michelle Dunavant	Linda Hutton	Dianne Papasan	Anne Stokes
Johnnie Amonette	Tommie Dunavant	Barbara Hyde	Maggie Phillips	Margaret Tabor
Mary Berol	Livia Dunklin	Calista Ingram	Selden Popwell	Pat Kerr Tigrett
Barbara Biedenharn	Andrea Edwards	Peggy Jalenak	Carol Prentiss	Deborah Dunklin Tipton
Judy Bowe	Michelle Ehrhart	Toni Kaiser	Missy Rainer	Ashley Tobias
Tina Butler	Katie Eleazer	JJ Keras	Alice Rawlins	Bridget Trenary
Kay Carey	Mary Ellis	Elizabeth Labry	Ann Reynolds	Cortney Viglietti
Karen Carrier	Allison Garrott	Chicken Lea	Mary Robinson	Marsha Wedell
Elizabeth Cates	Lynn Gayden	Debbie Lewis	Leslie Rothschild	Alison Wetter
Meg Clifton	Elizabeth Gillespie	Emma Lincoln	Elizabeth Rouse	Chey Widdop
Brenda Crain	Lucia Gilliland	Julia McDonald	Diane Rudner	Barbara Williamson
Allison Crews	Harriet Goshorn	Harriet McFadden	Sally Saig	Martha Witherspoon
Mimsie Crump	Dotsie Graham	Susan McGowin	Susan Schadt	Martha Wood
Carol Dell	Sarah Haizlip	Mabel McNeill	Bonnie Smith	Anna Wunderlich
Barbara DeWitt	Cynthia Hardoon	Abbay Milnor	Dina Smith	Jean Wunderlich
Katherine Dobbs	Gaye Henderson	Julia Montgomery	Susan Smith	Susan Wunderlich
Susan Dobbs	Martha Hester	Mena Morgan	Christy Snowden	
Libby Dorris	Liz Howard	Snow Morgan	Judy Snowden	
Anne Dunavant	Buzzy Hussey	Brandon Morrison	Terri Snowden	
Kelli Dunavant	Eva Hussey	Nancy Morrow	Karen Spacek	

www.wildabundancecookbook.com

Published in 2010 by
ArtsMemphis
575 South Mendenhall
Memphis, Tennessee 38117
www.artsmemphis.org

Photographs © 2010 Lisa Buser
All images by Lisa Buser except:
Images on pages 38, 40 (two images on top left), 98, 102,
129 (bottom) by Murray Riss
Images on pages 90 – 91, 93 by Michael Juiliano
Images on pages 246 – 254, 258 – 260, 264 – 273 by Will Smith

Text and design © 2010 ArtsMemphis
Designed by DOXA

Library of Congress cataloging-in-publication
data available

ISBN 978-0-615-39823-5

Printed in the United States by Four Colour Print Group,
Louisville, Kentucky